MY WIFE

& TIMES

Daniel Will-Harris

To request permission to reprint any portion of the book, e-mail *publish@SchmoozeLetter.com*

Library of Congress Cataloging-in-Publication Data

Will-Harris, Daniel
My Wife & Times
1—Humor, Marriage Anecdotes, relationships, lfacetiae, satire, etc.
1. Title.
HW734.B685   2002   306.8'5   87-3277

Some material in this book is based on material that has appeared elsewhere in another form.

Cover design by
www.will-harris.com

LOLchemy Press
www.schmoozeletter.com
Box 1209
Point Reyes, CA 94956

FOR TONI,
OF COURSE

CONTENTS

LOLchemy

Relationships   *11*

Work   *49*

LOLCHEMY

Shock to Shtick

"You're going to look back and laugh at this someday." That's something I tell myself on a regular basis.

These seem like particularly trying times—but you could say that at just about any point in history. Time passes, and inevitably somebody looks back and sees the humor in it.

It used to take me years to look back and laugh—but now in some cases I can do it just minutes after the fact—condensing the event down to moments that seem funny in retrospect.

It's one of the reasons I became a writer—so I could change reality, rewrite the past and change shock to shtick, transform tears to laughter.

I call it *"LOLchemy"*—a combination of LOL (the web acronym for "laughing out loud") and alchemy.

Once a moment is gone, all that's left is a memory or a bruise, and it's better to be able to look back and laugh.

RELATION-
SHIPS

GRILL THIS

Combustible

I don't know why, but I stopped wanting to BBQ a few years ago when my house almost burned down. No, it wasn't my fault, it was a nearby forest fire, but somehow after that, the idea of flames close to the old homestead have not been good for the appetite.

So recently when my wife wanted to BBQ, I said, "No, absolutely not, I forbid it," and the next thing I knew we were driving home from the store with a hibachi to BBQ on.

There we were, surrounded by a yard full of kindling, with a small fire-driven device, sure to spew sparks. And my wife couldn't have been happier. I warned her that if she burned down the neighborhood I was going to chase her down the street brandishing a tire iron. She was amused.

My niece, Ocea, helped me assemble the hibachi. Despite it being only 10" square, it was somehow designed requiring two people for assembly. The instructions involved some badly photocopied line drawings that looked like a schematic of the invention of a square wheel—or instructions showing how to attach a tail to an armadillo, it wasn't clear which.

I immediately did what I do best—put it together wrong, with the feet (small scraps of flammable wood) on sideways so that the thing could fall over, spilling white hot coals onto the flammable wood table my wife had chosen to hold the hibachi on our combustible wood deck.

After all this work, my wife's first words were "It's so small!" She was apparently unable to comprehend that a 10" square box that said "10" grill" would contain a 10" square grill. "I thought it would fold out or something," she informed me. "What about the picture on the box?" I asked. "I didn't think it was 'shown actual size'" she answered, having missed the words "shown actual size" printed on the box.

At one point my wife had planned on cooking four chicken breasts, four pieces of corn on the cob, and other assorted grilled vegetables—on her imaginary grill. Then it hit her that four chicken breasts by themselves would only fit if the chickens were midgets.

Now that it was assembled I noticed that the grill fit at an angle designed, I guess, to cause anything placed on it to slide off. This didn't seem conducive to cooking something for more than the time it took to slide off. "Can't you bend it?" She asked, as if I was superman and could bend cast iron with my bare hands. "No, but I have a feeling that when we put something on it, it will probably fall off, so don't worry."

Now came the time to "fire it up!" We'd bought a bag of Mesquite charcoal so that it would have that natural forest-firey flavor. But when we opened the bag we discovered that they were more like meteorites than briquettes—each piece of charcoal was larger than the entire grill.

"Can't we break them into smaller pieces with the hammer?" she asked, looking at me not as if this was a question but a command. Whenever she says "Can't *we* do something?" I know it means "Can't *you*?"

So I took out the hammer and hammered away but only managed to dent the charcoal. The head of the hammer, however, did manage to fly off somewhere into the garden. I was just glad it didn't go through a window.

We had thought the charcoal was the self-lighting kind, but upon closer reading of the bag, it said, "Just drop the whole bag into your grill and light the bag!" If we'd lit the bag our entire deck would have become the grill.

So now we had the charcoal in the dimension-challenged grill. For kindling, my wife used shredded paper from a box that had arrived through an eBay auction, as well as twigs and dried leaves that had fallen onto the deck.

This was when we realized that somehow everything on our deck was flame *retardant*—except, of course, for the deck itself. That's right, twigs and dry leaves, dried rosemary and lavender that should have gone up in smoke just sat there. Even the paper didn't burn.

A half hour went by and the grill was still only warm to the touch. My wife and niece insisted they could see a red glow. I feared it was the hibachi's wooden feet.

And then, after only about an hour and a half and a full lighter of butane, it was somewhat hot. Not white hot, mind you, but at least not cold. So on went the chicken breasts. Without a sizzle. We covered it with the old Weber cover (which could have covered four of these little grills). It was getting dark and cold, but at least we finally heard some sizzling, and the chicken was getting cooked.

My wife said, "When this is done you're going to tell me this was the best chicken you've ever eaten." I replied, "I've certainly worked up an appetite," as I hosed the deck off again.

Once we took the chicken off the grill my wife was going to douse the coals with the hose. I said, "Let me move away so I don't get covered with ash," and she said, "There won't be any ash," just as the ash exploded in a small mushroom cloud.

I made sure the grill was sitting in water, so there was no chance of a tragedy during dinner. And the result? It was the best chicken I've ever had.

SHELVING IT

Two Left Hands

My wife always thinks that the very next shelf I put up will, once and for all, end clutter as we know it. She sincerely believes this—until about three minutes after the shelf is up.

She admires the shelf—brimming with things, (many of which would have fit ever so neatly into the trash), then she looks back at the room and in a split second of horror, realizes *even she* can't even see a difference. Somehow we have filled yet another shelf and yet made no dent in the room's clutter quotient.

A few weeks later, after the shock's worn off, she'll see another sliver of space on the wall and announce, "That would be perfect for a shelf. It would really clean up this corner."

I have stopped cringing (though not sighing) because it does no good. The cycle has begun again, like the seasons. It's always the same. We go to the hardware store. She has me move dozens of very long and heavy pieces of wood until she finds one that has just the "right" grain. She exclaims, "I can't believe how expensive wood is!" as if she hadn't just bought another $25 board a few weeks earlier.

She says, "Should we put it in the trunk?," like our trunk's made of rubber and can expand to fit it. I say, "It

won't fit," and she says, "I can make it fit," and we try
and it won't. She'll then get it to fit into the car, because
she can get *anything* to fit into the car, which probably
explains her confusion about the trunk. I'll sulk while
driving home, because I know that one end of the board
is sticking into the padded panel behind the back door
where it will create a permanent dent.

The board comes home and "ages" in the garage for
a few days or months or as long as I can stall. One day
she'll remember and stain it. Then she'll say "Put it up
now—I've already done everything else!"

Some people say they have two left feet. When I do
home improvements I feel like I have two left hands. I
rarely find the studs in the walls, even with the help of an
electronic stud finder. So I make a lot more holes than
should be necessary and if I was smart I'd buy stock in a
spackle company.

Then I struggle. I curse. I fear that I've driven a screw
into an electrical cable that will light me up like a
flashbulb and launch me airborne off the ladder, my
skeleton glowing as if in a cartoon.

I inevitably realize I've put the brackets on upside
down, or in the wrong place and have to rip it out and
start again. If I do ever find a stud, then it's guaranteed
I've put the screw in the wrong place and won't be able
to get it out because the head is stripped.

If she's nearby she'll give me helpful hints to which I generally scream, "If you know so much why don't you get up on this ladder and do it!" It's never pretty.

Lest it get routine, each shelf has it's own surprises. Last week I put up an especially difficult shelf which had those hateful keyhole hangers in the back so everything has to be measured correctly (who's bright idea was that?). I finally got it up and put everything on it, then I made the mistake of closing the back door. This minor act apparently sent tremors down the hall which released the shelf from the wall, sending its contents flying.

To me, this just made the point I had been trying to make to my wife—it's time to hire someone to do these things. To her it just made the point that I needed to do it again—right this time.

Since there was no stud in the exact position required by the hateful keyhole hanger I'd used a molly bolt which either had neither molly'd nor bolted, but had managed to make a hole in the wall large enough stick your tongue through (I'm not saying I did).

Fixing this airy new addition to the wall took two entire days. I managed to lose three toggle bolts to the hungry wall; they were swallowed whole. I finally realized I needed a big toggle bolt and a washer the size of a saucer, which I actually found at the hardware store with the help of three clerks. I assembled the toggle, a hex nut, the washer, then the bolt, and voila, I now had something on the wall that could have passed for modern art in the 80's. If I'd remembered to put a wing nut at the end it would have been really good, but I figure it will stay up at least until it doesn't.

And now I just wait for the cycle to begin again. I'm seriously thinking about removing all the wallboard in the house and just using the studs as shelves. It'd save a lot of time.

IT'S CURTAINS

I've Seen The Light
And It's Not The Sun

I now have conclusive proof that dolphins are smarter than we are. The proof—they don't need curtains (or dishes or cars or VCRs or porcelain figurines for that matter). Clearly they must be smarter if they can live happy lives without all the stuff we "need."

I've come to that conclusion today because I'm in the midst of a "curtain trauma," as the evil decorating genius that occasionally inhabits my wife is trying to find new living room curtains to replace the ones she made 11 years ago.

I didn't think selecting some long pieces of fabric involved months of drama and intrigue, but apparently I was wrong (again). We are now on our third set of "window treatments" and these, too, have failed to pass muster.

You have to understand, these aren't ordinary drapes. These are "environmental enhancements" that not only have to look good but also keep out the "damaging rays of the sun." I didn't realize it, but, my wife has implied in uncertain terms that everything we have in the living room will dissolve into a pile of dust if the sun so much as touches it.

Now—I understand that direct sunlight can destroy fabric and carpet, yet somehow other people manage to make their belongings last without having to live in total darkness. Our unique solution has been for the design motif of said living room to be "Hibernation Bear Cave Chic." So even after 12 years, everything in the room would appear like new, if you could only see it.

One of the supposed purposes of the new curtains was to "make the room lighter." My wife always laughs at a TV decorator named "Hildy" who has a trick of saying she's making the room "lighter" while actually painting it black, but her style of decorator rhetoric seems to be infectious.

We first bought light curtains, a beachy beige and black canopy stripe that was the antithesis of bear cave. They looked great in the catalog and arrived looking like used medical gauze through which light streamed as if they were invisible. Ms. Mole did not approve. Those were mailed back.

My wife then explained that when she said she wanted the room to be "lighter" she was talking about the color of the curtain fabric and she didn't mean she wanted actual light entering the room. But of course.

Next we tried matchstick blinds—these would block direct sun but let the view and some light in. I thought they were great, but apparently too much deadly light was sneaking through and we needed something more "dense" (other than my head).

This lead to a loud public argument in a Home Depot where my wife insisted on bamboo blinds that I felt would be perfect for a trailer in Alabama but which didn't go with our living room. My wife explained that this would lend an air of "the English Bahamas" to our living room, even though the rest of the room was totally devoid of anything English or remotely Bahamian.

These blinds got home and once in the window were pronounced "dreadful" by the very person who'd chosen them (who shall remain nameless) so they went back.

I was starting to wonder it was a matter of taste. My wife and I have always had almost uncannily similar taste in things, so we don't have the problem that some couples do. There's a TV program called "Designing for the Sexes" where the man usually wants all chrome and glass while the wife wants English Country chintz and the smart decorator gives them something with no chrome but just a touch of glassy chintz so that no one really got what they wanted but his soothing tone made them believe they wanted beige art deco all along.

Yesterday new drapes (which were suddenly being referred to as "panels"), started to arrive, via eBay. They were beautiful Dupioni silk which you can buy at famous design shops for the price of food for a month. On eBay they only cost the price of food for a week. They were supposedly "taupe" but I thought they were green. I was huffily informed that they were "bronze," and went around thinking I had suddenly become colorblind until a few days later when a certain someone accidentally referred to them as "greenish."

They were quite beautiful in the package, and I even liked them in the window. My wife, however, was concerned that they let too much light in, and she didn't like the color or the texture. Other than that my guess is that they were perfect.

Now she has to sell them on eBay from whence they came, so if you're looking for luxurious greenish-bronze drapes that let in enough light to actually see in your room, just search for "Taupe Dupioni silk" and you can enjoy them too.

So it's back to the drawing board. I jokingly suggested gluing aluminum foil on the windows and was shocked by her delighted reaction. Perhaps I'll make lemonade by creating little pinpricks in the foil so it looks like stars. I am joking, of course. We'd never put foil in the windows. That would be too easy.

SOMETHING
FOWL

The Gates Of Hell, Always Open

It all started with a giant chicken. I am *not* making this up. If I hadn't seen the 12 foot tall fiberglass chicken, things would be much different today.

On the way to do some shopping I saw a giant chicken, in a giant coop, next to a little antique store.

As we whizzed by, I said to my wife, "Did you see that giant chicken?" Looking back it's amazing that she just said, "No, where?" as if a giant chicken was perfectly natural. I told her that it was at an antique shop we'd passed hundreds of times and she said, "I've always wanted to go there, but they're always closed. You want to turn around and go back?"

Well, see, right there I should have sensed trouble. My wife does not believe in turning around. I have never understood why, but whenever I say, "I can turn around" she says, "Never go back." It's one of those things that, from the tone of her voice, I've never even questioned.

If I'd stopped and thought, then I'd have realized I was making a u-turn into the Twilight Zone. I turned around in the driveway of a store called "Artsy Fartsy," (I swear I am not making this up, which makes it all the scarier).

We parked right next to this shop, which is never open, and oddly, it was open. Another clue that something was wrong that I stupidly didn't see. And I *should* have known better, too, because this whole little area has weird vibes.

A few years ago, just across the street from where we parked, there was an old store that one day went from being a shack to a palace, with bright Christmas lights all over, thousands of them, blinking all the time. We'd drive by at 2 am and it would be lit up, flashing, and *open.* It was very enticing, glowing as it did. We jokingly referred to it as, "The Gates of Hell, Always Open!" And we wisely never stopped.

But in the bright daylight, nothing seemed odd about a 12 foot chicken by the side of the road. It was like one of those horror movies where the people in the movie think everything's perfectly normal, and everyone in the audience is screaming, "Don't go in! Don't go in!"

And like the idiots in scary movies, we went right in. I asked the price of the giant chicken and was told it wasn't for sale.

Of course not, this evil chicken was placed there solely to lure poor unsuspecting eccentrics who, for some unknown reason, thought it might be fun to have a giant chicken on their driveway.

I added my name to a long waiting list of people who have probably all suffered something unspeakable by now.

I even supplied my phone number—who knows what horrors await me from that. Heavy breathing. Calls from telemarketers during meals. I don't even want to think about it.

We started to walk back across the gravel parking lot, and no sooner did I have the key in the car door when I heard my wife screaming, "Oh no! Oh, oh, oh!" I ran over to find her lying on the ground, writhing in pain, a cloud of dust swirling around her.

I looked for a giant chicken footprint next to her. But no, these giant fowl are too clever for that. I saw a truck backing up and wondered if she'd been hit (she's always walking behind cars that are backing up and I'm always telling her not to)—but maybe the chicken had just made it look that way!

I helped her up, but she couldn't walk and was in so much pain she couldn't talk, either—so I didn't know what really happened. I put her in the back seat with her feet up, and she told me to go get ice. I thought what I really should have done was to get some matzo meal and wave it threateningly at the chicken.

Even with ice, it wasn't long before her ankle looked like she was wearing a bagel anklet. Two x-rays later I was informed that would be months until she could walk normally again. As the doctor said, torn ligaments can take longer to heal than a clean break.

So the moral of this? Loose gravel and holiday shopping can be hazardous to your health.

And enjoy everything you can—even simple things like being able to walk.

And finally, think about having a really, really big *chicken* at your next holiday meal. That'll show them who's boss.

YOU DOG, YOU

Call Me "Puppy"

Lately my wife's been talking about getting a puppy. She looks through the online animal shelter listings and researches the personalities of various breeds—then she disregards all that and then chooses the one she finds most appealing.

She doesn't seem to realize she's already got a puppy—Me. I can do everything a dog can do—and more. Of course, maybe the "and more" is the problem.

I think the reason she doesn't get this is because most of the time I don't act like a puppy. Why not? Because she doesn't treat me like one.

No, she mistakenly treats me like an adult, which is, of course, always a mistake. If she insists on treating me like an adult, then what choice do I have but to try to act like one (notice I said "try to"). And what fun is that going to be for her?

I have tried, over our many years of marriage, to explain this to her. But her response is always something like, "I'm not going to be the only adult around here." Well, since she probably already is, why not just face the fact and get on with it? Then maybe she'll see the puppy in me.

I explain that if she'll only treat me like a puppy, instead of a man or Pit Bull, then I'd be a friendly little loveable cuddly puppy for her. I would even promise never to eat the sofa leg, or have an accident on the carpet.

But no, she just comes back with, "why do *I* have to be the one to change?" and then whole question becomes moot. She could be getting impressive results using nothing more than a dog training manual. Instead, she's falling into the whole "adult" quagmire.

When I was younger I used to think that people just turned into adults and never knew what hit them. Now that I've lived a few more years I'm fully aware that most people are fully aware of what's hit them, they just can't find people who'll treat them like they *aren't* adults so they feel compelled to *act* like adults, and there you have the root cause of most of the problems in the world.

Because (and this is the big "adult secret" that we're not supposed to tell anyone under 21, so if you're under 21 and reading this, make sure to pay special attention because this may be the only time you'll hear it) most people really are only *acting* like adults. Inside we're all like 5 year olds—immature and needy and doing really stupid things because of it. But we can't let "the children" know this, so they grow up and go through the same stupid cycle.

The solution, in this case, is in the hands of women. Yes, it really is. Women have to take the initiative because they are the smarter sex. It's kind of like noblesse oblige. I just read that the Y chromosome that makes men has only 1% of the genes X chromosomes have. Dr. David Page of the International Human Genome project called the "Y" "A rotted out version of the X." Well, that explains a lot, doesn't it? I personally find that a tremendous relief, not to mention a darn good excuse.

Maybe it's also our genes and prehistoric need to hunt that makes us appear active, while we're really just reacting—waiting for something to move so we can spear it and good look in front of the ladies.

As any lady should know, men are really more about *reaction* than action. It starts when we're babies. If our mother smiles, we smile. If our mother looks worried, we're worried. I saw it on PBS, so it has to be true.

Now, I know there are a few macho men out there (especially those too young to know better) who are thinking, "Hey, I'm the top dog. I don't need no b*tch telling me what to do." To those guys I say, "You're young. You'll learn. And don't use that kind of language when talking about a lady." If you're not young and you still think that, I say "maybe this explains why you're alone." To the gays out there, I say, "One of you has to be the girl."

Besides, that tough Alpha Male posturing is all fine and good among other males, but it simply doesn't work with the females. They may think it's cute at first, but then they find it tiresome.

Our idiot Y chromosome may be making us *act* as if we're the dominant alpha-dogs, but in reality we know we're just looking for someone to pat our heads and say "What a *good* boy! What a good *boy*!" I know it. You know it. Admit it, and let your inner puppy out.

So, ladies, when you look at a man, just see us as the animals we are. At our best we're beloved pets. At our worst, we're vermin. But we can't help it. We were born that way.

Woof.

COMPUTER LOVE

Symptoms of Life

I'm jealous of my wife's computer. She spends more time with it than she does with me. Sure, she knows how to press my buttons, too, but lately the computer has been getting more attention than I have.

Of course, she turned to her computer because I was already spending too much time with mine. She'd call me for dinner and 45 minutes later I'd emerge from my office (which she calls "the hole") thinking just five minutes had passed. She couldn't understand it. Then she got a computer and now she understands and does it herself. If I dare ask "What's for dinner?" I'm lucky to get an answer in 45 minutes. And we have popcorn for dinner more than really seems necessary.

Sometimes I have to e-mail her downstairs to get her attention. At one point she took her computer to bed, but that was simply too much. Now she just has it on the sofa while she watches TV, which is fine except when we're watching TV together and she's glowing brighter than the screen—it brings a new meaning to "she has that special glow."

But I can't blame her—I understand all too well. My computer is more than a machine. It's a tool, sometimes a faithful friend, other times an evil nemesis. Sometimes a window to the world, other times an escape from it. Virtually always mesmerizing. It's not nearly as smart as my wife, and doesn't smell as good, but it does what I say more often.

I'm aware my computer is not alive (in the traditional sense). Since it's yet to recognize itself in a mirror, it probably can't pass for sentient. Still, it has all the symptoms of life. It puts out heat. It makes noise. It responds.

I know how to turn it on. It lights up when it sees me. It's always there for me. It does what I ask, more often than my wife (who is editing this and would have cut that sentence out if it had bothered her). I can communicate with it using touch alone. It informs me and nags me. Assists and confounds. Helps me focus and distracts me. It knows my secrets and does my bidding. It puts up with me, puts out for me and gets put out with me.

Yet like all relationships, this one has its share of pain. Sometimes we have difficulty communicating. At times we even seem to speak different languages. Occasionally I can't understand what on earth it's thinking. I ask it to do the smallest thing and it acts like it's an ordeal. Often it just seems to ignore me.

And lately it's started to hurt me. My hand started aching from years of moving the mouse. It's done this to me before, and usually a few day's rest and a wrist-brace get me over it, but this time it wouldn't go away. It moved into my arm, my shoulder, and then into this muscle I'd never even known existed that ran up my skull and ended in a little knot at the top of my ear. And did the computer show any sympathy? No. Come to think of it, that's also like some people I know...

I bought a wrist brace—you know the kind—it's beige and looks a little like an medieval instrument of torture. Badly designed, with Velcro and badly sewn edges that worked like sandpaper against my skin. I took it back. The computer, apparently repentant, helped me find info on the web that lead me to *www.smartglove.com* which was far more comfortable and helpful (but has yet to answer a single question I've posed to it, so I do wonder just how smart it is).

Next, my computer helped me find a mouse-substitute, a trackpad like the kind on laptops. I find it natural and comfortable to move the cursor just by pointing with my finger. The last time I tried to install one, it caused my previous computer to have a total nervous breakdown. This computer suggested a USB (the relationship-saving-port) one that just plugs in and works, no drivers. Now I can use any finger to point (depending on my mood!). It's helping my hand heal, and the computer enjoys accessorizing itself.

So we're back on good terms—for the time being, at least. Come to think of it, my wife would probably enjoy a little accessorizing herself. I think I'll turn off the computer now and go press her buttons.

GENETICS: SCIENTIFIC KARMA?

A Sum Of Their Parts

I have my father's laugh but my mother's sense of humor. My mother's temperament and my father's temper. My father's mouth, with my mother's taste.

I think about all this because my birthday is just a week away, and that always reminds me of where I came from, and where I hope I'm headed.

See, I think of genetics as "scientific Karma." We are who we are when we're born—a concoction of the family that came before us, and hopefully a little more than just the sum of their parts. While we all make decisions that define our future, we always make them based on who we were born.

I mean no disrespect to my parents, both of whom are fine examples of the human genome, but I do sometimes wonder whether it was such a good idea for them to mix their genes. I sometimes feel that *before* they made me they broke the mold.

I shouldn't complain, because if it wasn't for them I wouldn't be sitting here typing this, nor would I have ever discovered the joy of texts. Or trees. Or chocolate for that matter.

And I certainly can't blame them if their genes were a little like oil and Jello—good ingredients on their own, but a questionable recipe when combined. This could explain why I've been called "an acquired-taste." (I just know they're both going to e-mail me and demand to know which one is Oil and which is Jello, but it's just a metaphor!)

This could also explain why I am a Gemini. My wife has suggested that Dr. Jekyll and Mr. Hyde were Geminis, but I just ignore her. Or I throw things. While I inherited many fine traits, there are times when my Gemini-like nature makes me feel like Siamese twins who each want to go different directions.

So when my birthday comes around, I ask myself, "What am I going to do about me?" I know that sounds kind of selfish but I can't change anyone else, so I might as well try to improve myself.

(To balance out any selfishness, I ask people to donate in my name rather than sending me gifts—this applies to everyone except close friends and family, who I tell exactly what I want, just as I've been doing since I was five—it eliminates those "Oh, wonderful — argyle socks!" disappointments. As I've said, this year I want a big solar panel to use during our so-called power crisis.)

So I'm going to forgive myself for not being all those things I'm *not*, like tall or thin or able to leap tall buildings in a single bound. And I'm going work on learning to accept myself for who I've always been—I might as well—I haven't fundamentally changed since I was five—what makes me think I'm going to change radically now?

(Once again, my wife chimes in to say I sometimes still act like I'm five, and she's right. What she doesn't say is that she acts like she's 16, which isn't necessarily that much more mature.)

In the end, we're all kind of like the John Malkovich in "Being John Malkovich." We have countless little pieces of our ancestors inside us, trying to tell us what to do.

In the ever-present battle between Nature and Nurture, I always bet on Nature. While parents want to believe that they can somehow prune their children into little topiary shapes of their choosing, in reality, kids are who they are, and parents just need to avoid snipping their little buds off before they can bloom.

(P.S. My wife wishes to state for the record that the above quotes are what I, the emotional-five-year-old heard, rather than what she, the 16-year-old, really said. Nya nya nya . . . blah blah blah.)

MOM'S ONLINE

95 Years Ago, Last Sunday

My mother used to be unable to work a clock radio. Now she's reading e-mail and working the web. If that isn't an indication of how pervasive the web is, I'm not sure what is.

Why? Because mom was born 95 years ago (last Sunday). Not really, but that's her story. While most people adjust their age to make themselves younger, she's always taken the clever tact of claiming to be 25 to 30 years older than she really is so everyone who sees her will say, "You look so young!" It helps that she bears a resemblance to Elizabeth Taylor and has an unforgettable personality.

I think the reason she claimed not to be able to work a clock radio was that it was a good excuse not to set an alarm. She's always been good at logic like that and has been a constant inspiration when it comes to seeing the world from a different perspective.

For example, when I was little, she invented the "between meal snack" not just as a treat, but as a way of life. It took years for science to catch up and claim it was better to eat a lot of small meals than a few big ones. When I was sick, she let me sleep on her mink stole, redefining luxury. She always felt that you could learn more from real life than from a class, so as a kid I won the "worst attendance record" award in school, while at the same time I could identify a Frank Lloyd Wright building, a painting by Monet, a sculpture by Claes Oldenburg, and every model of car on the road.

When she went back to college, she had me study with her, so it was like I got to take college classes when I was 12. In high school, when I wasn't doing well in one class, she blamed the teacher instead of me. She went to every show I was ever in, and sat in the audience saying, "That's my baby!" (just a little too loud, but that was OK).

And she gave me lots of good advice:

- Enjoy today, you could be hit by a bus tomorrow.
- Eat something good, you'll feel better.
- Be open to everything except infection.
- Pickles count as a green vegetable.
- There'd be no reason for all those big football players to fight if someone would just buy them each their own ball.

She's managed to survive everything that life has thrown at her. She may not have passed on the world's healthiest genes (you can't have everything), but she's passed on something more important—spirit. So, what's the point of all this, other than scoring points with my mom?

First: sometimes people think that there's no one over 30 on the Internet. The truth is that there are people in their 80's and 90's on the web—I know, because they e-mail me, telling me things like how they've built their own computer. (Hey, they could build a crystal set, why not a computer?) Mature people appreciate the web more than kids do, because they can remember the world without it. (I know kids who can't remember the world without remote controls and personal computers).

These days a lot of companies focus on teens because they figure a teen can be a customer for a lot longer than a grown-up. But adults are more loyal to brands—and they *need* more help, because even though teens have all that angst, adults actually have it harder.

Second: Every once in a while it's good to stop and remember that your parents had a lot to do with the *good* things about yourself (not just the bad :)

Third: E-mail your mother. She's sitting there, by her computer, waiting. Who'd have believed it?

E-MAIL FROM
THE BEYOND

Long Ago, But Not Very Far Away...

I'd never really thought about it. About where messages go when you send them on the web. About where messages come from before they get to you. About where they might be, in time and space.

I'd never even thought of the simple things—like when you write an e-mail, or post a web page, or read a web page, that it's running down the phone lines, down your street, into your house. And before that, those tiny bits and pieces—invisible, are zooming around the globe, sometimes into space on satellites. You can't see them. You can't feel them. You can't hear them or smell them. It's like they're in another dimension that just shows itself to us through our computers. All these things are happening now, that 100 years ago, people would not have believed. It would have been science fiction. Or occult.

So I didn't think anything was odd when I received the following e-mail:

"Hello, Daniel. You probably don't remember me, but I was at the hospital when your father was born. I recently got into the internet and while I can't get around much in the real world, I realized I could go anywhere in

cyberspace! I found you and wanted to make contact!,
Love, Gertrude."

Wow. It was like being transported back in time. I
thought about the new connections that are being made
around the world, and though time—like synapses in the
brain. As if our world is getting more and more
connected, and maybe with more connections we can
create a new world while at the same time staying
connected to the old one.

I forwarded the e-mail to my father, but he didn't
answer. He was on vacation somewhere. It was either a
cruise to Afghanistan, or he'd gone to China for takeout. I
lose track of his real globetrotting, as opposed to my
virtual globetrotting.

Despite getting over 100 e-mails a day, I wrote back to
Gertrude right then, as if time had stopped for me. I said
how amazed and delighted I was to hear from her, and
how exciting it was to talk to someone who had seen
the entire century. And how I wished I could meet her in
person. She wrote back:

"In the past, if you couldn't meet in person, you
couldn't meet. So we wouldn't be meeting now. But
that's changed, and we are meeting, and while I don't
think we can meet in person just yet, I am pleased to be
able to talk to you again after all this time.

"I was alive before there were automobiles, electric
lights, refrigerators, even the telephone. Now people

grow up and think these things are natural, like trees, they can't imagine a world without them. But other than time going so much faster than it used to, I think people still *feel* the same now as they did back then."

I wrote her that I was born before remote controls, VCR's, microwave ovens, cell phones and personal computers, but that's not quite the same. Her e-mail made me think about everything we take for granted. I asked her to send her picture, if she could.

"That's not possible, for so many reasons, not the least of which being that what I look like is not what I feel like. I feel like time stopped when I was much younger."

We had many e-mail discussions. She told me about her childhood growing up in Cincinnati, Ohio. About how she was married in 1922 to a wholesale candy maker in Charleston West Virginia. About how she moved back to Cincinnati and had a real estate business with her husband. She wrote about my father as a child. And about meeting me when I was a baby. (Sometimes I forget I was ever a baby, even though I sometimes still act like one.)

I felt like I knew her and that we had made a special connection. I wanted to meet her. "You already have!" she wrote back.

My father came back from wherever it was he had gone and I e-mailed him asking if he'd received my mail

about her. He said he'd never received any forwarded
messages from me. I decided I'd better call—that way
I'd *know* he was getting the message.

I told him about all this. I told him about Gertrude
and when she was born and married and where she
lived. He was silent. I could feel this odd chill—even over
the phone.

You couldn't have gotten that through an email.
"Gertrude was my mother," he said. She died when you
were a baby.

After we hung up, I searched my e-mail. There it was.
I looked at the return address. I looked up the domain.
There was no such domain. There had never been such
a domain. I went to print out the e-mail to send it to my
dad, but my computer said the hard disk had a bad
sector. My backup e-mail file was a week old—before
she wrote. I never received e-mail from Gertrude again.

Here's to interesting e-mail.

RUMORS

Press Released

DATELINE: REDWOOD CITY, CA. Daniel Will-Harris, responds to rumors that he is planning to merge with eBay. Will-Harris states, "I don't comment on rumors."

Will-Harris says, "It's true I use eBay a lot, so I can see how the rumors got started." Behind the scenes, other indicators have led pundits to mull a merger. Will-Harris explains, "Yes, my wife has 173 positive feedbacks on eBay, which explains why our house full of stuff and the source of the cardboard box avalanche in the garage. But I do not have "eBay envy" and would not consider merging just so that my wife would return my e-mail faster."

"What's more, there are no plans to auction myself, or even my stunningly beautiful yet invisible-to-the-naked eye collection of nano-figurines celebrating the invention of the shoe tree."

Will-Harris continues, "Stock and merger mania has gotten out of hand. You can't watch cable without a stock ticker scrolling across the bottom of the screen. I was watching a rerun of "Friends" and when Monica made chocolate chip cookies, there was a news flash saying that Hershey's stock price had jumped two points. This was wrong on so many levels, not the least of which

being that *http://www.ghirardelli.com* makes the best
Double Chocolate Chips."

Will-Harris took this opportunity to refute other
rumors, "No matter what you've heard, I am not dating
Charleze Theron, and despite evidence to the contrary, I
am not the love child of Xavier Cugat and Charo. I know
that if you close your eyes I could possibly bear an
almost uncanny resemblance to them, but if that's the
case, then open your eyes!"

Finally, Will-Harris states, "Just because we might
buy a new 2-line phone doesn't mean we're also buying
Lucent (do I hear another rumor starting?)." In other
news, Mr. Will-Harris' chinchilla *is* looking for another
chinchilla to merge with.

WORK

I AM NOT A COMPUTER

Silicon-Based

My wife always says, "No one on their deathbed ever said, 'I wish I spent more time at work.'" This is something I can attest to first hand.

But how quickly I forgot. The last few months I got so caught up with a new project, that I started to feel like a computer. And I didn't like it. The chip on my shoulder was a Pentium.

A 14-year-old once told me, "If you enjoy it, it's not work." And he was right. Which explains why this new endeavor I was involved with felt so much like work.

I blame computers (it's easier than blaming myself.) While computers let you be more independent—they also lure you into spending more time working. They make it easy to forget about the idea of "office hours" when you're in your home office. The computer doesn't need to sleep, so it called to me, nights, weekends, 3:30 in the morning.

Computers let you telecommute (good), but they can also make your coworkers think of you as "just an e-mail address" (bad). That, and the fact that you can get more done at home, can cause coworkers to treat you as if you were a machine (bad squared).

In this particular "new project," my co-workers never met their deadlines because they'd come to think that everything I did was instant because I made the mistake of working very hard and very fast.

It didn't matter to them that they were two days late in supplying me with the material I needed to complete the job. Surely I could finish my complex tasks in minutes because I had a fast computer.

I got to the point where I couldn't stand having *my* buttons pushed 18 hours a day. So I did something I haven't done before. I unplugged myself.

And suddenly, I was happy again. I was human again. I could see the sun shining. I could smell autumn. I was back in the real world. One of the things you learn when you work on your own is that some jobs just aren't worth the money. Somewhere along the way I'd forgotten that. So now I'm poorer, but wiser—and happier.

So are *you* feeling silicon-based, instead of carbon-based? Take this handy quiz:

- Do you spend more time with your computer than with your family, friends or pets?
- Have you started to say, "I don't have enough bandwidth" when you really mean "time"?
- Do you feel like you could use a few more gigabytes in your brain?
- Are you "always on" and do you do such a good job that your coworkers take you for granted, like the computer on their desk?

- Have you forgotten where your off-switch is?
- Is it hard to remember the last time you took an entire weekend off?
- Do you talk to your computer? (come on, admit it, I know you do).
- Do you *yell* at your computer? (of course you do).
- When you take a break from work, do end up on eBay?
- Do you find yourself looking at chainsaws online for cutting down phone and power polls?

Here's your score:

If you answered "yes" to:

- All ten: You need to be unplugged.
- Six to nine: Find your off button, and use it.
- One to five: You are in denial. Get therapy—offline.
- None: You are in the Matrix. Try to feel the back of your head.

As things get faster and faster, there's still only so much a person can do. Remember, while computers can run 24/7, people can't. So blame your computer. It won't mind. Say it crashed. Take a day off. Enjoy life (while you still can).

And finally, a quote I just read and liked:

You can't direct the wind,
but you can adjust your sails.

Once I became human again, I was able to stop working and watch the Miss America contest (they stopped calling it a "pageant" and tried to pretend it was a game show). I have a long history of always being able to choose the winner, just from one look at the beginning of the show. This year, my choice, Miss Louisiana, came in second. Clearly they made an error tabulating the votes. Or maybe the accountant just wasn't a computer :)

FIRST YOU
PANIC

Dryer Lint Of The Stars

Every time I start to design a new project I secretly fear I've forgotten how. So when I started to design *www.schmoozeletter.com* I decided I would write down my steps along the way:

STEP 1: **Panic.** This is always my first step. My mind races. I start to wonder if it isn't time to find a new line of work—I try to think of new careers for myself, which proves a pleasant procrastination procedure.

This time I came up with stunning new e-commerce concept: *Dryer Lint of the Stars.* Even the famous have dryer lint—but unlike you and me they also have fans who will pay top dollar for it. I know I would pay for Meg Ryan's. According to casual calculations made while actively avoiding work on the site, I figured that just one of her bulky sweaters would yield approximately one framed portrait in lint; a half a dozen hand-made lint-paper note cards; and 12 lint-puff key chains sealed for posterity in non-yellowing acrylic.

If you're thinking, "He has finally cracked," then you are so very wrong. If I was cracking would I think you'd think that? OK, maybe, but I have it on good authority (my wife's) that I haven't cracked, I just have occasional difficulty with the concept of reality.

Now, why would stars give up their precious lint? Cash, and lots of it! And perhaps the hope that some fan also just happens to be a geneticist who can clone them from cells in the lint, extending their career. If they want top dollar, they can even contribute belly button lint!

See, I've thought this all out quite thoroughly and already have my first sale of Marisa Tomei's lint. My friend Ernest has offered to pay and now all I have to do is locate Marisa's laundry. My friend Karen has said she'll notarize it to prove that it's legit, and I think I can hire my wife, the unofficial "queen of eBay" to handle auction.

So I'm all set! Well, I am as soon as I meet Marisa. So if you know her, tell her I need to talk to her or do her laundry, either one.

STEP 2: **Come back to reality.** I rarely like this part, unless I imagine that I will win the lottery. But that doesn't really count as reality, so this should give you a clue as to my state of mind.

STEP 3: **Ignore the advice I give to others:** I do this to save time. Then, days later, when I realize that I haven't done much else other than look at watches on eBay and am perilously close to actually buying a non-working "Radium Swatch" that features an actual x-ray of Madame Curie on it, I come to the conclusion that I've wasted a lot of time.

STEP 4: **Do what I tell other people to do.** I force myself to answer the same hard, important questions that I force everyone else to answer. This part can actually be fun and exciting, but concentrating hard on anything requires a lot more physical effort than most people give it credit for, and therefore requires adequate napping.

STEP 5: **Reconsider lint.** I look at what I've done and think it's either embarrassingly bad or outright terrible and imagine that a blindfolded child with the hiccups and an Etch-a-Sketch driving over rocks in a Jeep without shocks could do better.

STEP 5: **Snap out of it**. This is often accomplished by throwing out what I've done and starting from scratch.

STEP 6: **Come up with an idea.** It helps to be hit by a staggering bolt of inspiration at this point. Unfortunately, your chances of this are just slightly higher than that of being hit by a lightning-fast Ford Pinto.

Since inspiration eluded me, I had to actually be logical and realize that since I already had a personal caricature/logo I've used since my first site opened in 1995, I could use that. The difference this time was that since the SchmoozeLetter can jump around from seemingly random points until it finally makes a picture, the logo could reflect this with a kind of "connect-the-dots" look.

STEP 7: **Ignore it for a while**. The only way to clearly see something you've created is to put it away for a few days. As long as possible, in fact. Then I glance at it, quickly, pretending it was designed by a total stranger. If my first impression is, "I'm glad I didn't design this piece of..." then I know that something went horribly wrong along the way. If, however, I feel jealous of myself, I'm probably on the right track, creatively if not psychologically.

STEP 9: **Show it to people you trust** but who won't be hurt if you totally ignore their advice. Apparently, my wife trusts me a lot.

STEP 10: **Always have a step ten**.

TRAFFIC JAMMING

In Your Dreams

Lately I've been having some really odd dreams. I enjoy them for the most part, even if I do sometimes wake up feeling like I've been up all night at Mardis Gras.

I won't go into the dream about the five foot tall denim-colored rabbit, or the one where a child swallowed Julia Child (creepy, I know, and if you're a psychiatrist and afraid for my sanity, feel free to write me).

I'll just tell you about the dream I had two days ago because I think you might find it useful. (I'll skip the beginning, where I'm looking around Martha Stewart's bathroom, amazed that her shower is as big as a locker room and doubles as a bumper car rink, complete with white and gold gilt bumper cars in styles ranging from rococo to Jetsons.)

Here's the useful part: I'm in the wings of a theater (the wings are the area to the left and right of the stage, areas the audience can't see). I'm watching the performance on stage—Don Johnson (who is a musician in real life) is rehearsing a kind of dance/mime play. People are in a long line, with big pieces of cardboard on their sides, and it's clear they're supposed to be driving on the freeway, stuck in a traffic jam.

They get out of their cardboard cars in unison, pull out cardboard musical instruments, and start to play. The group has created a "happening" where musicians are invited to drive onto on crowded freeways and when the traffic stops, they get on top of their vans and jam.

They are jamming traffic to promote awareness of conservation—showing that traffic jams are a big waste of time and energy. They want to encourage people to telecommute, which efficient and easy.

They get lots of press coverage. Trafficopters flying overhead get the perfect view of the group's name, painted on top of their vans, and transmit it to the evening news. Soon the group starts making and selling CDs they sell on freeway onramps, donating the proceeds to the non-profit group, "Traffic Jamming."

Smart marketing—it's entertaining so people like it, it costs nothing, gets a lot of attention, and is memorable later on, every time someone's stuck in traffic.

I'm watching all this from backstage, drinking ginger/bacon tea (it's a dream, I can't explain these things) and thinking, "That's a great idea, I wish I'd thought of that."

Then I woke up and realized I *did* think of that. And I wrote it down on the pad next to my bed, so that I could remember it..

I think it's important to listen to your own ideas—no matter how stupid they may sound at the time.

The thing is—everybody has ideas, but *most* people don't listen to themselves. We all spend years listening to other people tell us our ideas are no good, and sometimes we start to think other people are right. Well, what do *they* know? There's no harm in *having* the idea. Write it down. Maybe you'll use it, maybe you won't. Maybe it will lead to another idea you *will* use.

Let the idea age (like fine wine or cheese, but a lot faster) and see which ones still sound good in a day or a week. Then tell other people about it. Don't be upset if people try to tell you all the reasons why your idea is impractical, if not impossible, or just plain stupid. They may be right, but it's *just as likely* that they're wrong.

Most of the inventions we use every day wouldn't be here if the inventor had listened to the people who told them all the reasons why things wouldn't work. It works both ways—next time someone tells you their idea, first try to think of how it *could* work, instead of the other way around.

So excuse me—I've got to go put my guitar in my van. OK, so it might help for me to buy a van and learn how to play the guitar—but at least I know the first steps. That's how it starts. Watch for me playing in traffic. Film at 11.

One More Thing: Dream on

I used to write down all my dreams, but now I only write down the ones I remember when I wake up. Unfortunately sometimes my writing can be, well, illegible.

For example, here's all I can read from last night's dream: "shore of acceptance, big beach nugget lots of people a king of big bath in Sumor all the time surprise! Diane Sawyer."

I do remember it was about beach houses that were made of those huge aluminum cargo containers you may have seen on giant cargo ships, and come to think of it, that's not such a bad idea for emergency shelter!

Then again it's starting to sound as if I need professional help, isn't it? Involving either psychology or graphology...

DANCING
BEHIND A TREE

Schlepping Your Way To The Top

In a previous life (meaning before I was married), I was a dancer. I still am a dancer, actually, only now I only dance when no one's looking.

I used to perform in musicals like "Hello Dolly!" and "The Music Man." When rehearsals started, choreographers would inevitably put me in the back row. At one point, my dance partner and I were actually placed *behind* a large potted palm.

Now, from that you might think that I *wasn't* a very good dancer—but, in fact, I was—I just didn't look like a dancer. I didn't have a "dancer's build." I was thick and had a plumber's build.

I also wasn't a *natural* dancer—I started out being such a klutz I made those dancer's in the Charlie Brown Christmas special look good. I looked kind of like I was having some kind of a fit.

It was a long time ago, so I can now admit that I was really, *really* bad when I started. So bad that when I'd audition, I would actually hide behind the curtains in the wings of the stage, hoping no one would see me.

But I worked very hard and overcame my natural inabilities. I learned to compensate by using personality over technique. After shows people would tell me that it was hard to watch anyone else. I chose to take this as a compliment. Even Angie Dickinson and Valerie Harper told me this (OK, so I'm dropping names, but it was a big deal for me).

I didn't get anywhere as a dancer—show biz can be very much about how you look so choreographers would never put me front and center. I'd dance fine, but they didn't want anyone getting a very good look at me, as if I might embarrass them because I *wasn't* anorexic.

I didn't like being in the back row. I doubt anyone wants to be on the stage yet hidden. So I took it upon myself to correct their error in judgment, and move myself to the front of the stage.

Maybe because it was more important to *me* than them, but after a few weeks I'd have worked myself up to the front. As other dancers missed rehearsals, I'd be there (I never missed a rehearsal), in their place. I don't think I really fooled anyone, they just kind of got used to it.

By opening night, I'd be front and sometimes center. I used this same technique repeatedly on many shows.

My friend, Kelly, turned this into an art form. You can see him when you watch the movie "Grease." He's the blonde one who constantly manages to get himself *between* John Travolta and Olivia Newton John.

I was in a singing/dancing group for many years, and during that time I learned how to "sell" a number. On stage, "selling" has less to do with how good a singer or dancer you are, and more to do with how much energy and enthusiasm you have.

I learned that if you forgot the words or the music or the steps, if you just *smile and bounce* the audience doesn't really notice (or care) what you *haven't* done. They just want to be entertained and smiling can get you a long way (just look at Julia Roberts—a fine actress to be sure, but her smile made her famous).

So, *when in doubt—smile and bounce.* (No, you don't have to look like you're ready to be committed, there are different ways to smile and bounce, most *not* involving tap shoes.)

What I learned from all this is that you have to make your own opportunities. When you're stuck in the back row, move yourself little by little to the front. It may take time, but you can do it. And once you're in the front row, act like you belong there.

MY 15 MINUTES

Extra, Extra!

It really was a dark and stormy night—the night I was in my first movie, a memory brought back by last week's Academy Awards.

The movie was Halloween II, and my wife and I were "extras." Extras are the people in the background who are kind of like props with legs. If they do their job right, you never notice them.

It was a "night-shoot," so we arrived at 8 p.m. It was already dark, cold and wet. Because extras are at the bottom of the movie making "caste system" (think "untouchables"), there weren't even chairs for us to sit on. They expected us to sit on the cold, wet curb for three or four hours *in the rain* until they were ready to shoot. My wife was appalled by this.

Since she's never afraid of authority figures, she soon spied a prop police car and she suggested we get in where it was dry. I thought this was a *very* bad idea. Before I knew it there were six of us huddled inside the car.

I was terrified that an AD (assistant director) would find us, send us all home without pay and yell, "You'll never work in this town again!" I only stopped worrying when I fell asleep, along with the everyone else in the car.

We woke when someone banged on the hood and pointed towards the catering tent, because dinner was being served at midnight. Since everyone else had eaten, we lowly ones could eat what was left. We clambered out of the car and had a surprisingly good dinner.

Around 3 a.m. the rain stopped, the lighting (which always takes hours, even when it's not raining) was done and they were ready for the first shot. We were an angry mob (shades of irate villagers with torches in Frankenstein) throwing rocks and stones at the infamous Halloween House. It sounded like great fun until we were cold and unable to feel our fingers which made it difficult to throw rocks well enough to break windows.

We stood in front of the scary-looking hovel which was just a badly maintained house in an otherwise nice South Pasadena neighborhood. The AD informed us that we were angry (duh), and we wanted the guy with the hockey mask out of the house! Of course I can't imagine that we wanted him coming out *at* us, but they never give extras much to go on.

The lights switched on, as bright as day, but made to look like night. The director and camera rose on a crane in the middle of the street. The AD yelled "Quiet, people, this is a TAKE!" and then we heard "action" and we started throwing rocks and stones at the windows.

The thing we weren't doing was yelling, because 1) it would upset the neighbors, and 2) they would add *professional* yelling in post-production.

They replaced the glass in the windows and shot the scene a few more times, then moved on to a scene with Donald Pleasance talking to police men (extras with moustaches) while we milled around directionless in the background.

At around 6 a.m. they paid us $20 in cash, and we went home. Months later the movie came out and we're on screen for about a second. You can see my wife because she's cleverly wearing a snow white coat. You might be able to see me because I'm overacting right behind Donald Pleasance.

We did extra work on a few more movies, including a big three day stint on a Dyan Cannon TV movie where she spent one entire day yelling the same line, "Dace, Jess!" until it was burned onto our brains (clearly it still is!), and we discovered our that new friend, "Chalet" a beautiful, tall African American woman who worked in the garment center location, was actually a man. Shades of Midnight in the Garden of Good and Evil.

My career as an extra skyrocketed to include such impressive non-speaking parts as a hot dog vendor on the TV show Cagney and Lacey (the crew said they were very impressed because my acting was "so big" it could be seen from across the street).

My last, and I mean last, extra job was a few years ago when John Carpenter was filming "Village of the Damned" in our small town. It starred Christopher Reeves (who's acting was brilliant in person—he was also extremely nice off the set), Kirstie Alley (the less said the better), and Mark Hamill, who said I could have read his wallet if he hadn't lost it.

After three long nights filming (at a big $40 per night), my appearance on screen consists of my left arm. My wife's role is bigger—her ear has a tantalizing brush with fame as the camera glides by.

My favorite review of this movie was, "Village Of The Damned is one of the worst movies I've ever seen—everything about it was bad." Well, surely not my wife's ear or my left arm.

THE COLOR OF DIGITAL MONEY

How Green Was My Bankbook

I still don't quite understand how money works. I remember my mother taking me to open my first bank account. I only wanted one because when you opened an account, the savings and loan gave you a coin bank in the shape of a Ford Model T.

I handed over my $5 and in return the nice teller presented me with the car, and a little blue bank book. My mom got up and we were leaving and I said, "Where's my money?"

The teller said, "In the bank." I shook the toy car bank and heard nothing. I started to get cranky. "No it's not," I said, getting all teary-eyed. "It's in *our* bank," she said.

I looked at the car. I looked at her. I looked at the little blue book. And then, at the top of my lungs, I screamed, "I gave you five dollars and all you gave me was this stupid little book!"

The young woman explained that they kept my money for safekeeping, and when I wanted it back, all I had to was show them the book. It sounded like a racket to me. I showed her the book and said I wanted it back—now. She said, "all right, but you'll have to give me back the book and the car."

My brain froze. This was too complicated for a five year old. Money. Car. Book. Book. Money. Car. What did these people want from me? I wanted the money. I wanted the car. And now I even liked the little blue book because it was the littlest book I'd ever seen and it had gold stamped on the cover.

I decided to outsmart them all. I'd take the book and car now. Then I'd come back tomorrow and get the money. I put the little blue book in a place so special I immediately forgot where it was. But I loved the car and still have it in a box in the garage (which, given the fact that we have a couple hundred boxes, is like saying, "It's somewhere in the state of California").

My wife will tell you that my grasp of money hasn't improved much since then. I know if you do something people want, then they'll give you money. And I know money is necessary to get toys, but that's about as far as my comprehension has ever progressed.

It must be even more confusing for kids today. Often there's not even any actual money—just numbers on a screen. You can probably understand that. But what about kids? How hard must it be to understand that you can type $20 in one place and it means nothing, but if you type it in another it means you get a genuine birch wood model of a T. Rex?

When young people (it makes me feel old to use the phrase "young people") ask me how to get their start, I tell them to start by trading. Build a web site or do some work for a local restaurant or store in trade for food or toys (though I tend to say "peripherals" which is an adult word for toys). Not only can you learn a lot by working directly with a local business person, but you get something tangible out of it, not just some numbers on a screen.

Because, as little as I know about money, I do know this much, courtesy of Thornton Wilder's play, The Matchmaker: *"Money is like manure. It's not worth a thing unless it's spread around, encouraging young things to grow!"*

NORMALCY

Unlike Everybody Else

When I was a kid, I just wanted to be normal—like everybody else. But I wasn't normal, as kids around me constantly pointed out. My hair was curly when everyone else's was straight. I was "husky" (the nice word for it) when all the other kids were skinny. I liked Broadway musicals when other kids listened to heavy metal. I didn't play baseball, I played Legos.

Before second grade started I insisted on a Beatles haircut. My mom obliged, and when I walked into school (I can still remember it clearly) I looked around and realized to my horror that no one else had a haircut like mine. The rest of the boys mostly had crew cuts (which I called "toothbrush hair"). They all looked like "Dick" in the "Dick and Jane books," and there I was—a mop-top fab four, age seven.

I was, in short, different. And I didn't like it. I spent many years trying to fit in. Trying to be like everybody else. No one was fooled, not even me. And then, since I was a lemon, I finally started to make lemonade. I stopped trying to be "normal" and started to enjoy being an individual.

I wore different clothes a (interesting old suits from the thrift shop, and anything else that I liked). I worked unusual jobs. As a teenager, I was the Nurseryland Bee. I stood on the sidewalk dressed in a big bee costume and tried to attract customers driving by in cars. What I mostly did was cause traffic accidents, scare adults (kids weren't scared) and almost pass out from the heat.

I bought an unusual car, an AMC Pacer (which is still on my driveway, only now as a kind of non-kinetic sculpture). I thought (and still think) it's beautiful. I put eccentric and fun things in my house. Next to my computer monitor is a stuffed toy elephant hanging like King Kong onto the top of an aluminum model of the Chrysler building (and I don't care who knows it!). I didn't do any of this just to be different, but because this is what I liked, and I wasn't afraid to show it.

When I started to write computer books, I decided they shouldn't be like other computer books—high-tech and boring. Mine were funny and looked elegant. They were different and they sold well.

What I learned from all of this was that being different makes your work stand out. While that's terrifying as a kid, as an adult, it can be a big advantage.

While being different may mean that *some* people may not like you, being boring means *no one* will. If you're different, chances are more *will*.

Lately I've worked for some people who, despite being adults, are still *afraid* to be different. These people range from late 20's to late 40's, and they're still acting like they're 14—as if being different is the worst thing in the world. They point to other company's designs and want to look just like them.

I *say*, "If you're just a copy of them, why should anyone be interested in you instead of them?" I *think*, "Grow up!" Of course, I could be more mature myself if I wanted to. I just don't think it's a such good idea.

IT'S AN E-GOOD THING

Martha Imperfect

Martha Stewart never replies to my e-mails. I don't blame her, I know she's busy. But I've never been one to let reality stand in my way. So here, without further ado, is my interview with "Martha."

DwH: Martha, how do you get so much done?

MARTHA: Well, my first time-management tip is not to sleep too much. I sleep two hours a day. I know you love to nap but you can't manage a billion dollar Omnimedia empire that way.

DwH: I don't have a billion dollar Omnimedia empire.

MARTHA: And now you know why. Here's a little time-saving tip—simply fly back and forth across the international dateline in order to gain extra days!

DwH: My friend Pete just flew from San Francisco to Australia and completely missed Thanksgiving day. Went right from Wednesday to Friday.

MARTHA: He crossed the dateline from the wrong side.

DWH: Ah, of course. How silly of him.

MARTHA: I see that your computer monitor is going undecorated this holiday season. Simple sprigs of holly, snipped from a neighbor's yard, can do wonders to cheer up a computer monitor. You can buy a charming

Monitor Holly Holder on my site! I've redesigned my web site (well, it wasn't me personally, it was one of my little designer elves), so that now everything points to the store.

DWH: I did notice. I was trying to find a cookie recipe and all I could find were your cookie cutters for $49.95. It was hard to tell the exact price, because the type was so miniscule. Not a good thing.

MARTHA: Elves are very small, hence the type size.

DWH: But I'm not an elf.

MARTHA: More of a North Pole Troll, are you? They're small too. Love tiny type.

DWH: No. And I am having a hard time reading your site and finding anything but ads and links to buy things.

MARTHA: See, elves and trolls simply adore that kind of thing.

DWH: Don't you think that most of your site visitors are *not* elves or trolls?

MARTHA: I believe we're all elves and trolls at heart. Except for me, I'm queen of the elf-trolls.

DWH: You and my wife, both. Look, I have the highest regard for you and find you fascinating, in the way that Marie Antoinette was fascinating...

MARTHA: We sell a bedspread styled after one used by Marie at Versailles for $99.99 in twin.

DWH: But where's the useful content?

MARTHA: All of my items are labeled as per international law. The bedspread is 100% combed cotton.

DWH: I mean the content on your site. I can't find it.

MARTHA: We don't want to give too much away.

DWH: And your site's hard to navigate—I don't know where to look.

MARTHA: Think like a gnome, then.

DWH: Now you're starting to annoy me.

MARTHA: A Noel Faerie would never say that.

DWH: I am not...

MARTHA: Many of the people on my staff are Faeries. Not that there's anything wrong with that.

DWH: Do Faerie's like to sign up for your e-mail newsletter on November 30th and get an e-mail offering 20% off, then read in that same e-mail that the offer expired November 9th?

MARTHA: That's why it's so important to use that international date line crossing tip. You're clearly not my elfish demographic.

DWH: You are driving me batty now.

MARTHA: You like Bats? I sell Halloween products!

DWH: Sigh.

HEALTH

A MINOR PROCEDURE

Bump In The Night

The human body is a wondrous thing. Mine certainly never ceases to do new things to amaze and frighten me.

It used to be I'd go the doctor for every little thing. Then I married. And my wife would say things like, "So you can't open your right eye today. You'll probably be able to open it tomorrow..." and "There's nothing a doctor can do for that broken toe, just walk it off, Kippy..."

When I'd try to argue with her, she'd say, "And where did you go to medical school?" Since I didn't go to medical school I felt I had no argument. It took me years to remember that *she* didn't go to medical school, either—not that it mattered.

So last week when a bump the size of a walnut appeared overnight, I didn't say anything about it. Well, not for about eight hours, at which point I felt compelled to show her the bump the way I sometimes feel compelled to ask her to taste bad cottage cheese, just to confirm it's as bad as I think it is.

When she immediately said, "You should see a doctor about that," I figured the worst. I thought of the movie "Mask," and imagined that within 24 hours I'd be unrecognizable to anyone but Cher.

By the next morning the bump of mystery was even bigger, and harder, as if the tooth fairy had turned mean and embedded a stack of quarters under my skin.

My wife got a doctor's appointment for the same day. Now—you have to understand that my wife can get a doctor she's never met to give her prescriptions over the phone. No one, not even the doctor, know how she does this. So getting an appointment on a Friday when the doctor is only there half day was like child's play for her.

I thought the doctor would only look at it, poke it really hard so it hurt for days, then say, "Go home you cry baby." So imagine my surprise when the doctor prodded it, *measured* it, and called in three nurses to look at it, as if I had a goiter in the shape of the Virgin Mary.

The doctor told me to lie down immediately (as if the bump might somehow be throwing the earth off its axis). Then she and the nurses hovered over me, aiming bright lights in my eyes, as if to disorient me. I heard the doctor say, "You'll feel some slight discomfort," right before she stuck with me a needle.

"Can you stop for a second and tell me what you're doing?" I managed to bleat as the doctor said, "Hemostat, stat," and the nurses busied themselves waving what to my confused mind appeared to be ritualistic herbs.

I felt like they were either getting ready to throw me in a volcano—or roast me under the hot light like the chicken I was.

The doctor finally spoke, "It's nothing. We're just going to remove it." I'm thinking to myself, "well, if it's nothing, why do you have to remove it?" I envisioned the doctor pulling out her trusty hacksaw while I bit a bullet like some Civil War soldier. She repeated, "It's nothing, really. Whatever you do, just don't move now."

While I didn't technically pass out at this point, I basically chose to ignore consciousness. Looking back, all I remember is the bright light and what seemed like an "alien probe," but I have conveniently forgotten the details. "OK, all done," the doc said. "If that thing that looks like elbow macaroni falls out, which it probably will, don't worry about it. I'll see you in three days."

And then they were gone, as quickly as they arrived, except for the nurse who was nice and smart enough to realize that when I tried to get off the table in the middle of the procedure I wasn't trying to get fresh.

She shaved my chest (which seemed a little forward since we'd just met) and covered me with what felt like a marshmallow and duct tape. Then she left with a little piece of me in a small vial, either as a memento or a biopsy, I wasn't clear on which. I sat up, dizzy. The bill seemed quite reasonable which made me wonder if they had secretly taken a kidney as a trade-in.

My wife wanted to go to lunch, which I did because I was still in too much shock to say, "Can we go home now?" And after lunch we went shopping and she took advantage of my altered state and bought 11 pairs of socks.

EYE YI YI TEST

Testing 1, 2, 3...

I can't help it—I cheat on medical tests.

I don't mean the kind they give in Med school—I couldn't be a doctor because I get nauseous easily—even by things as minor as the wrong kind of tuna.

I mean the kind where they poke and prod and probe you in every existing orifice, and some new ones they create just for the occasion.

There are some medical tests you simply can't cheat on. I've yet to figure out how to lie on a blood test. Or look at the blood of the person next to me and copy it. Can't be done as far as I know. My friend Karen, who's such an accomplished liar that she considers it a sport, couldn't figure out a way, either. So other than giving them someone else's blood, I'm pretty sure it can't be done.

The reason I cheat is because I find many of these tests annoying, if not downright rude. A few weeks ago I'd taken a normal eye exam of the "which looks better, this way... or this way? This way... or this way?" kind. This test is simple and they didn't have to stick anything into me, so it almost got my seal of approval.

The problem was the typeface they use on the eye chart, which, frankly, is a poorly designed face where the

"O" looks nearly identical to the "D" so it's all too easy to make mistakes on that test. It's not my eyes, it's poor typography. I don't think it's fair to give people poorly designed tests. I felt that about the SAT test, and I feel that about eye exams.

Today I took a "field of vision" eye exam. It's designed to tell the doctor how good my peripheral vision is. My peripheral vision is just fine, but I don't take chances with my eyes, so if the doctor says, "you should take this test," I start sweating and wheeze, "Why, what's wrong?" and agree to anything.

This test is one more of those things where you have to put your chin on this holder thing apparently designed for orangutans. It doesn't fit any human chin, except perhaps Jay Leno's. Then you put your forehead against a rubber bar that countless other people have put theirs against and it has no protective paper of the kind you put over toilet seats and right there I'm finding this unacceptable because I don't know where other people's foreheads have been—and I'm getting queasy just thinking about it.

Once in position you must look into this blank white half sphere—like one of those giant Imax movie screens, only re-sized as if to show movies to mice. Looking at this thing is like having temporary snow-blindness. I can't focus on anything, which makes me dizzy right off the bat, and then it's so blank my brain starts making up stuff to see so I don't go insane.

In the middle of this unnatural orb is a small dark circle containing a yellow light glowing mysteriously like a HAL 8000. As I stare at this, tiny almost imperceptibly faint dots of light jump around the screen. Each time I "see the light" I press on this little buzzer thing that looks like someone stole it from the set of Jeopardy.

And, oh—did I mention they've covered one eye with a black leather patch apparently ripped from the face of Blackbeard the pirate? And the room is like 90 degrees.

So I'm already annoyed when the tests begins—and it's hard *not* to cheat. Every time the light flashes there's a faint click of the projector moving. It moves once every two seconds. The clicking seems to have a kind of like a Samba beat, so I want to press the button in time to the rhythm. So maybe it's a good hearing test, or a reflex test, but it seems like a poor excuse for an eye exam.

I'm sorry—white dots on a white background? With one eye closed and the other staring into endless whiteness I start seeing things that look like ghosts with unruly hair. I finally realize that it's my bushy eyebrow which is sticking down in front of my eye, pushed there by the black elastic of the eye patch.

I ask the nice woman to stop the test, which she does. I explain I am seeing things and she says everybody does, but then I point to my eyebrow and she goes, "Oh, that." I say "Does everybody hate this test as much as I do?" and she says, "Usually more."

So it's back to the test. It's really hard to see the dots because my brain is so busy creating non-existent patterns on the whiteness so I have something to look at. I have to blink a lot otherwise the lack of motion makes everything kind of twinkle, then disappear. I'm sure this means I have some kind of personality disorder where my eyes must constantly be entertained because my ancestors were hunters. This is news, as I thought they were jewelers.

It's so annoying I find myself clicking the button even if I'm not sure I've seen any light. Each time I press the button it makes a loud click, though sometimes it makes two which makes me wonder if the machine knows I haven't really seen anything and am just mercy clicking.

Now I become unsure as to whether I'm seeing spots in front of my eyes, or seeing the little bitty flashes. It can't tell the difference, so it's not really cheating, it's more like an inability to distinguish between imagination and reality and I didn't need a test for that, I *know* it's always been a problem.

Then there's one horrifically long span of time where I hear the clicking but see no light and so I imagine I must have a blind spot the size of Drew Cary. (In reality, everyone has a blind spot where the optic nerve attaches to the eye, so I guess if I'd cheated too badly the blind spot wouldn't have shown up and they would have thought I was either a liar or an alien).

After eight torturous minutes I hear a buzz that sounds like a smoke detector has gone off adjacent to my forehead, and the test is over.

For that eye.

Now it's time to do the other eye.

As I pull my head away I notice that there's a glare off a piece of metal on the right side, which explains one of the white lights I saw constantly. How can they expect me to see nearly invisible lights when something that I'm not supposed to be seeing is glaring like the sun off the back window of a car? I think I should get extra credit on my peripheral vision test for this.

The test on the left eye is easier because there's no glare, and I've given up trying to see the light. If I think I see a flash I press the button. I assume that I'm actually seeing something, and if not, my imagination is sufficiently vivid, and that is a good enough substitute for reality—at least it has been all my life.

The first eight-minute test seemed to take 80 minutes, and this one seems to breeze by in a mere 40. The woman running the tests says the results look fine. I find it hard to stand, but I am eager to leave the little room, even if I'm madly squinting and blinking.

I stumble into the waiting room and my wife looks at me and says, "You're not going to drive like that, are you?" I say, "I'm fine just as long as it isn't snowing."

FOR WHOM THE
SCALE BEEPS

Weighted average

I lost five pounds this week. Without even trying. What's my secret? Well, I'd tell you, except I've always thought I could make millions if I ever combined the most popular book genres into one and wrote "The Mafia Quick Weight Loss Diet Mystery."

Unfortunately, I'm really bad at keeping secrets, and besides, this diet is so simple that the book would only be one sentence long, so here goes:

I call it the *"My wife's on a diet Diet,"* and it simply involves having your wife go on a diet. This automatically puts you on one, too.

I don't believe in diets. If you saw me you'd probably say, "Well, that much seems clear." But I just think diets don't work.

Yes, I can lose weight. I've lost enough weight to create a dozen David Duchovney's. But I've always managed to *find* the Davids again—plus at least one Olson twin.

I also believe that people, like dogs, naturally come in different sizes. No one expects all dogs to weigh the same, so why do all those stupid weight charts expect people to weigh the same?

Besides, people weren't designed with supermarkets in mind. Or TV commercials. Pay attention and you'll see every diet ad followed by a pizza ad. On one single night of "Must See TV" *every* show had the characters eating pizza *and* brownies.

This all plays on our animal nature that's constantly telling us to stock up because who knows when we'll eat again. I mean, it might be *hours.*

So I spent my time accepting myself, rather than reducing myself.

See, ever since I can remember I've been what I like to call "larger than life." Or "Above average in weight." Or at the very worst, "the ideal weight (for a taller person)." I avoid the word "obese" because it sounds so awful even "junkie" sounds better (the FDA and pharmaceutical industry seem to think so).

I now prefer "husky" which sounds kind of sexy. And my current favorite is "chubby" because a seven year old girl recently said to me "You can't be very old because you're chubby like a baby." I *love* that.

Then, last week, a box arrived from eBay. That's a normal occurrence around here, but instead of something decorative and useless, it contained something ugly and useful—a horrifying electronic scale that not only flashes your weight but then has the sheer unmitigated gall to tell you what percent of your body is fat. I was stunned. I checked the address to make sure it wasn't a mistake. It wasn't.

"I'm on a diet," my wife announced casually. The words went in my ear and out my open mouth.

"Diet? But... but..." I said, as articulate as I could be in a state of total shock and disbelief.

"It's not to lose weight, it's to help us avoid having massive coronaries," she calmly explained in her best Doris Day voice. There's no way to argue with that.

She handed me the scale. I touched it and it started beeping as if it was frightened. I knew now for whom the scale beeped.

"I'm not getting on that thing," I proclaimed. I don't want to know. I'll just get depressed if it tells me that I'm over 100% body fat," I exaggerated. I could still feel a few bones, like an elbow or knee, so I knew there were bones in there somewhere and I couldn't possibly have over 97% body fat).

"It's not for you, I don't even *want* you to get on it" she smiled, nonchalantly, knowing that not allowing me on it would ensure that I'd have to secretly try it.

I finally remembered to close my mouth as she left the room with her "lunch," which consisted of a few raspberries.

This just wasn't like her. This was the girl who had chocolate ice cream for breakfast. The woman who claimed cream was the source of her ever-youthful complexion. Butter's best friend.

She'd always been immune to the unhappy, pasty-faced dieticians glowering from the TV news, proclaiming things like, "eating movie popcorn is like injecting motor oil directly into your veins" or "deli food is like putting a corned beef to your head and pulling the trigger."

"How'd they get to you?" I asked, worried they might get to me. "Well, I had these pains... they were probably just indigestion..." she began at which point my brain started screaming "if *I* had an odd feeling in my chest area I'd be at the doctor faster than you can say 'EKG.'"

I regained my hearing just as she was saying, "So I went to the library and checked out every diet book" and realized by this time she'd probably already become a diet Rosetta stone.

Suddenly, all the diet doctors she made fun of were gurus. As she told me about the various diets designed to clean out your arteries I heard what sounded like distant thunder; it was my stomach rumbling.

"I'm hungry," I said. "You can eat whatever you want," she said, with a saint-like smile. And true to her word, she never told me what to eat. She also never made anything to eat. And that's the key, right there.

And yes, I did finally succumb to the scale. Before I stepped on the hateful thing I cleverly set it to Kilos so the number it displayed would be a lot smaller than pounds.

And no, I won't tell you what that number was, or what percent of my body is fat (though I will admit the possibility that a large percentage of it is in my head).

So I've lost weight, something I haven't revealed to anyone else yet because I don't want to hear them say, "You look *so* much better now," as if I had looked awful before.

My wife says we'll live longer. Personally, I think it will just *seem* longer."

SOME ASSEMBLY
REQUIRED

What a Workout

The UPS guy can get to my house in his sleep. Why? Let's just say that if someone on TV was selling life-size stuffed walruses, within weeks, one would appear in a cardboard box big enough to require a license plate, and shortly after that, it would be gracing our living room.

I bring this up because I just spent the morning, no, wait, it's almost 4 p.m., putting together something that arrived a mere two weeks after my wife ordered it on TV.

I'm used to a parade of small boxes arriving at the front door, containing things we clearly cannot live without. Inside are usually small, easy to lose things like tiny enameled eggs designed in the style of Marie of Rumania (I kid you not). I don't mind these, because anything good enough for a queen must be good enough for us. And mostly because no assembly is required.

So I was stunned a few days ago when I opened the front door. Instead of the usual box too small to hold a severed finger, I was greeted with a box big enough to be buried in. When I tried to move the box, I momentarily thought there might be a person inside, because that's how much it weighed.

I went back into the house and stared at my wife with one of those Ricky Ricardo faces that says, "What have you done this time, you crazy redhead!?" My wife gave me one of those eye-batting, "Whatever do you mean, darling, and aren't I sweet?" looks and said, "You look so handsome today!" which immediately made me suspicious.

"What did you buy?" I asked. "When?" she replied, honestly. "I don't know, but it's just arrived in a box that's taller than I am, so I'm hoping you didn't buy me a casket."

"Let me make your favorite breakfast," she cooed, changing the subject to something irresistible like waffles. She smiles beatifically, looking twice as sweet as pie. Now I knew I was done for.

But it's hard to be angry when you've been stuffed with waffles (and yes, I watched her make them to ensure she didn't slip in any special ingredients from a Lucrecia Borge poison ring). It was then she broke the news.

"It's a Pilates exercise machine," she said, precisely timed so that my mouth was too full to speak. I swallowed hard. She'd bought exercise equipment before and it always fell into one of two categories. 1) Dangerous, like the piece of black plastic you slide back and forth on that should have been banned by the Geneva Convention as an instrument of torture), or 2) Unused—well, that's not completely true, because becoming a place to pile clothes wasn't *completely* useless.

"I promise to use it every day," she added, quickly. "And I'm Marie of Rumania," I replied. She looked as sincere as humanly possible and continued, "I will, I promise, and this will save us a lot of money!"

Now, you have to realize that my wife's sense of economy is based on what I call Lucynomics—the economic system used by Lucy Ricardo on "I Love Lucy." If she bought two dresses and they were on sale at a savings of $20 each, she didn't spend money, she just saved $40.

"Just two sessions with a Pilates instructor would cost more than this entire machine." She exclaimed, with the studied excitement of a talk show host. "And if I don't use it every day, then we can return it."

Well, she had me there, yes, we could always send it back. It would only cost about $200 for shipping, or I could drive to Missouri where it came from, but at times like these there's no sense bringing logic into the conversation.

So I carried the box upstairs, or at least I tried. See, I have this thing about exercise equipment—I'm sure it's all very useful, but I've always felt that pushing around a vacuum cleaner is probably *more* exercise—and it accomplishes something useful, too.

The box was so heavy and bulky, that I soon realized
how it worked. All you have to do is lift the box and try to
move it. Talk about weight training! This works your
biceps, triceps, quadriceps, octiceps (and I didn't even
know I had those).

There are no complex exercises to learn, just move
the box, and in five minutes you'll get a workout
equivalent to lifting a Toyota.

But the fun had only begun. The box was sealed with
tape that looked like something they'd use on the space
shuttle to keep the cargo bay closed. It *had* been
shipped halfway around the planet, so I could
understand this, but I couldn't understand the giant bold
warning: Do not open this box with anything even
remotely sharp." What was I supposed to do, lick it until
the tape softened, and then use a butter knife?

Since I wanted to get it open without losing a lot of
saliva, I used half of a scissor and carefully cut through
the tape, all the while wondering if I was, at the same
time, slashing some kind of upholstery.

But they had placed cardboard under the opening (a
piece large enough to double as a porch), so unless I'd
opened the box with a chain saw, the contents would
have been fine.

Now came the fun part. The machine was all black
metal and looked like the cross between "the rack" you
see in horror movies, and various parts that might fall off

a Stealth Bomber. There were many pieces, and a big bag of nuts, bolts, washer, and things that my vocabulary lacked a name for.

My wife said that the people on TV said that the manufacturer said that you only need to screw in four bolts and you were ready. I think they lost something in the translation, and maybe the word "four" meant "seventy two" in another language.

And then came the instructions. One page featured a list of parts that should have been in the box—enough washers to assemble a rack-and-pinion power steering unit, and several large Frankensteinian bolts.

I carefully laid all the pieces out on the diagram, only to find that I had roughly half the pieces they said I should have had. But if I stopped every time some assembly procedure looked terribly wrong, then I would never assemble anything, so I forged ahead, hoping that the instructions were wrong—no, *knowing* they were wrong, because they always are.

Then there was a diagram with 72 numbered pieces and lots of arrows and the letters A through P with more arrows showing what pieces went in what holes. The written directions, however, mentioned things like M8 and NyNuts (honestly), none of which were shown on the diagram. Since my idea of a nut is a pecan, I wondered if the Yellow Pages has a listing for "assembler."

At times like this I realize that this is some giant psychology test, and I have to use my cognitive skills to figure out which thing fit in what hole. So I started at the end with the pulleys and tried to work my way to the end with the bungee cords and along the way I stuck in whatever would fit.

One of my family mottos has always been, "If it doesn't fit, force it," so at least I had an overarching theme from which to work. My proudest moment came when I realized that one of the tubular mystery pieces was actually a rudimentary wrench head. If someone had been watching, I'm sure that they would have seen a light bulb appear over my head as I realized that I could place a silver metal stick into one of the holes on the side and achieve leverage.

I was so proud—like a chimpanzee discovering how to use monkey wrench.

But no one was watching, because no one is allowed to watch when I assemble something. Otherwise they make suggestions and say things like, "You've put that in upside down" which makes me furious, even if it is usually right.

Since there were a number of holes that were underneath and inside various other pieces, I discovered entirely new positions I was previously unaware my body could make. I could feel the burn in my wrists, and when I felt dizzy I just draped myself across the thing, even if that meant that bolts were pressing into my kidney—clearly a new form of acupressure.

What a workout!

Now Bungee cord "Y-me" needed to be stretched and placed in convex clip "O-gz." This required more strength than I had, but I realized since running the car into the garage wall and ripping off the rear view mirror I needed to complete this task to somehow stabilize my marriage karma. So I found an inner reserve of strength and pulled like my wife depended on it, and voila, it was done. It was also in the wrong slot, so I had to pull it out and do it all over again.

After rigging more lines and pulleys than were needed in a summer stock production of Mutiny of the Bounty, I was done. Except for the extra bolt, which didn't seem to fit anywhere except in my pocket.

I sat on the bench which now slid back and forth smoothly, unless your foot slipped, in which case it slammed back with a force that could give you whiplash. I know this from experience.

I then discovered that the entire thing needed to be moved into the center of the room in order to have enough space to operate, but we didn't need a bed anyway, and this padded bench is pretty comfortable when you're on the verge of passing out.

Don't worry about me. I am resting comfortably now, and the machine's built-in traction settings mean that my legs can be held in mid-air so that blood can return to my brain.

When I regain the ability to stand, I will drive to Washington D.C. and suggest a new protective device to be installed in all televisions. Just like the V-chip that shuts off the TV when it encounters a violent program, my proposed E-chip would shut off the TV when any e-commerce infomercial or home shopping service came on screen. This would prevent certain people in my home who shall go nameless from buying anything else.

LOST & FOUND

In The Land of the Lost

I've lost my glasses. So if I've made spelling errors here you'll understand. Text on-screen looks kind of like I'm viewing it through the same misty lens that shoots Liz Taylor perfume commercials.

I've looked everywhere. Well, clearly not everywhere or I would have found them, because they must be here somewhere. I haven't looked under the bed... wait, I'll go look.... Nope. Lots of interesting things (thankfully none of them alive) but no glasses.

I do have *some* glasses on. They're so old and big that I look like Elton John unplugged—a scary thought. The frames are clear plastic with a kind of pink tint and the lenses are so big they cover my face from forehead to upper lip. Thankfully, the prescription isn't as strong as what I need now, so I can't see exactly how stupid I look. What *was* I thinking when I bought them? I must have *thought* they looked good. I guess other people didn't notice because they'd been overcome by polyester.

I can't find my *real* spare pair, which have the right prescription. I can only find this old pair I no longer want and keep meaning to donate to people who don't mind looking like they're ready to boogie. Oh—if my real spare is missing, maybe I *can* find my regular ones.

See, I have a theory about lost things. I believe there's
some kind of "Dimension L" (for lost) where things go
for a little vacation from dust and us. At least one thing
we own always has to be in this special dimension at
any given time. Luckily, this doesn't seem to be the case
with files on my hard disk (wait, I'm knocking on wood, I
don't want to tempt fate).

So while looking for my glasses, I've found many
things I lost and looked for without success in the past
and no longer need. I don't know why I *can* find things I
don't want—but *not* those I *do*. Why don't I throw most
of this stuff out? I have a dream of putting a dumpster in
front of the house and throwing things directly out of my
window, like in a wild French movie called "Betty Blue."
Wait—I thought my Chap Stick had gone to the nether
regions of time and space so I bought another, now here
it is, looking quite relaxed and fresh, and maybe even a
little tan.

I can find these things that were previously lost,
because my glasses have, apparently, taken their place
in the "Land of Lost Things." I hope they're happy there.
I also hope I lose something else soon, perhaps my car
keys (they always seem to enjoy a good rest) so that I
can find the glasses again.

OK, the trick is to look for something else. I know—
I'm going to look for a notebook filled with notes I make
in the middle of the night using the pen I bought that

lights up with an alien green light. Naturally the notebook should be right by the bed but no. That's good!

Maybe I was trying to decipher the contents which, in the morning light, tend to look like some dead language. Ah, here it is, too bad. I was hoping it would be gone, so that it could take the place of my glasses which would mysteriously reappear on my desk where I know I left them. But wait—the pen is gone. That's a good sign. Now maybe there's a chance to find the glasses.

I know—I'll find them the last place I look. Isn't that an idiotic saying—of course I will, because once I find them, I can stop looking!

Maybe I left them somewhere near the shower. I don't wear my glasses in the shower because there's nothing there I need to see clearly, in fact, it's better if I don't see anything in there clearly.

Nope. OK, now I've sacrificed my alien pen and still no glasses. I'm just going to give up—that'll be very Zen of me. Once I stop wanting something so badly I can find it. I think while I'm at it I'll stop wanting to win 60 million dollars in the lottery.

And there they are. Under a stack of mail I'm now throwing out. I looked through that stack three times, and, well, it doesn't matter, there they are. Now if I could only lose something else so I could find my spare pair. No, I'd better not press my luck.

At least I know where everything is on my hard disk (and when I don't, a simple Start/Find can locate it for me). And I back up every day so I don't lose anything (you should be backing up, too, before you have to learn the hard way).

While losing something in the real world is annoying, on your computer it can be devastating and mean weeks or months of lost work. Most people only seem to learn this hard way, by losing something vital. Don't be one of them. Now, If only I'd backed up a spare pair of glasses...

I wonder if, when you lose your mind, you find everything else. That's just a thought—I'm not willing to try it just yet.

ALMOST TWO
DIMENSIONAL

Near Death = Closer To Life

Last week was interesting, if you don't mind almost being killed.

Very exciting story. I'm on the driveway, taking out the trash (hence the excitement) and a big tree crashes to the ground, only inches away from me. It was like a fast cut in a movie—first nothing, then a crash, limbs, bark, a soft cloud of dust and silence. A second earlier and I'd have been a stain on the driveway! At one with the asphalt! Flattened like a cartoon character under a steam roller! And who says I don't live dangerously?

But "almost" was the most important part. I didn't die. I wasn't even hurt. Just kind of stunned. OK, very stunned. But since I was totally unscathed (physically) in some ways it shouldn't matter that this even happened. But because I can imagine what *might* have happened, it did matter, and it made me think, "You're *always* taking your life into your own hands." Every day you live, you have cheated death. Reason enough to celebrate.

I also thought I might go blind. No, I'm not a hypochondriac (though my wife might argue that point, even though when she gets a headache she immediately thinks "brain tumor"). I woke up and my eye was all wonky. Puffy. Weird. I'd never seen anything like that on anyone, much less on myself. I felt like a pirate, sans parrot. So I went to an ophthalmologist who said I had a "cold in the eye," and that it was going around. So it was like a stuffy nose, only in the eye.

Big deal, I know. But just like we often "don't know what we've got till it's gone," sometimes *thinking* you might lose something is enough to get the effect, without actually having to lose something. Much more convenient.

With this "good" news, I spent the rest of the day actually *seeing* things. I don't mean hallucinating, I mean actually *seeing* things—noticing things I looked at all the time but never really saw. Light. Leaves. Clouds. Pavement. Plastic. People. Everything *looked* different—because I was paying attention.

And these things made me truly thankful—rather than just taking things for granted, like we usually do.

So I have a wish for you this Thanksgiving (for those of you outside the United States, it's a popular holiday here in the US where you pretend to recreate the Pilgrim's first feast in "the new world," by getting together with friends and family and basically eating until you can hardly breathe, then falling asleep).

I wish that you will appreciate all you really have. It's cliché but true, that if you have your health, you have what's really important. If you have friends and family you're even luckier.

And if you read this on the web, it would mean you are part of the newest "New World," of the internet. You don't have to leave your homeland and ride on some creaking damp little boat across uncharted oceans. You can sit at home, in your underwear, and use this New World to help yourself create a whole new life, free of the tyrannies of the past.

So appreciate your health, friends and family, and the fact that we all have this new world to explore and stake a claim in. Hopefully, we can all use it to help make the old world a better place, too.

NEAR TECH EXPERIENCE

When Tech Equals Death

Maybe the universe is trying to tell me something. Not that long ago I was almost crushed by a tree. It reminded me to respect nature. Now I was almost asphyxiated by my new high-tech stove. All I have to say to the universe is, "You're confusing me!" First, you don't want me to go outside. Now you don't want me inside. I mean, what's left—another dimension?

I didn't do anything wrong, except trust a "new improved" stove. I bought it because I wanted the latest and greatest, and I made the mistake of actually using it straight away rather than waiting for the manufacturer to get feedback from other people and fix it. Let that be a lesson to me. And you.

It all seemed safe enough. I was boiling water for some herb tea (see, not even any caffeine) and I turned off the burner, or so I thought, and went back to work.

I don't have the best nose in the world. I mean, it's attractive enough, as noses go (if you think about them too long they're all kind of odd, and whatever you do, don't look at your feet for too long... ugh). But my nose could have a sign that says "closed" on it, since it often is. In fact, I don't believe I actually smelled anything until

I was 18. I didn't know I was allergic to cats, and we had 2, which meant I wasn't really able to un-stuff my nose until I left for college.

So I didn't notice anything even as my house was becoming what can best be described as "the old Hindenberg place on the corner."

I got kind of dizzy. And I coughed. But hey, it was allergy season, or, at least for me, it's *always* allergy season.

Then my wife, who has quite an attractive and effective proboscis, said to me, "Why do I smell gas?" and I thought, "Well, all I've had today is some toast, that can't possibly... oh, maybe she means like the gas that comes out of the stove... hmm, now that she mentions it, I do smell something odd, but I thought it was my Tai Chi clothes . . ."

So I dizzily stumbled to the stove, discovered I was just a click away from eternity, wisely decided against trying to "burn off" the gas by turning on the burner, and we scrambled around, madly opening windows.

What gets me about this is that it's so often the really stupid stuff that does people in. You hear about people falling out of airplanes at 30,000 feet and getting a few broken bones, but surviving. Then you hear about someone falling down in their own living room, hitting the corner of their coffee table and boom, they're dead. (Of course, those may be *evil* coffee tables.)

I'm fine, and hopefully the wiser for it. I learned that I probably should spray that allergy stuff up my nose, because we don't have a sense of smell just so we can say, "Hmm, I love the smell of bread baking."

I learned, once again, that the latest isn't necessarily the greatest, at least not until a few things have exploded and people have complained and little nagging bugs like that have been fixed.

And mostly, I learned that it's probably not dictators or space aliens or comets, or even high-cholesterol that's going to get most of us—it's life. *Life is, after all, the leading cause of death.*

RESOLUTION
DEPENDENT

New Millennium Resolutions

It's the new millennium. And we're all still here. Well at least most of us. I'm not saying we're "all here," I mean, my wife often says I'm "not all here," so why should I expect more of you? But if we're *not* living in the moment then at least we're doing a good impression of someone who is.

So, since the power is still on and food is still in stores (if not your refrigerator), then it's back to the normal New Year routine—making resolutions you have no intention of keeping then feeling guilty about not keeping them and eating ice cream.

But now there's added pressure. We can't just make a New Year's resolution, but also New Century and New Millennium resolutions, too! Where will it end!

My personal resolution is to lose weight by the end of the century. I'm pretty sure I can manage this if I'm not too specific about details. Also, losing weight really isn't a great resolution, being healthy is. But I digress.

My mother called saying that she saw on TV that I'd live to be 150. I'm not sure what I was doing on TV in Arizona without my knowledge. But maybe it was just "people of my generation" rather than me in particular. I can only hope.

Personally, the only way I think I'll see 2105 is as a brain in a jar with electrodes. And that's my idea of a bad hair day.

But who knows, maybe there'll be brain transplants by then, and I'll be able to stuff my brain into a clone of Ricky Martin. It could happen. Of course, all that wiggling might lead to the need for hip replacements, but again, I digress.

OK, so brain transplants are out, which means I'm relieved of having to make new century and millennium resolutions. But I do have some resolutions for this year:

- Focus on attaining my lifelong dream of being named Motor Trend's Sport Ute of the year.
- Eat only foods that begin with the letter C
- Go to Sweden and find out what a Sport Ute is.
- Come up with new names for bread and pizza that start with a "C"
- Establish lasting world peace.
- Learn English as a second language.
- Produce La Traviata with computer animated rodents.
- Find a publisher for my "Wallet Reading" book (unfortunately, this one is not a joke).
- Become a Solid Gold dancer.
- Protect the oysters of the world.
- Be kind and loving. Yadda yadda yadda.

That about covers it.

CIRCADIAN RHYTHM
KINGS

The Lost Track of Time

The clock by my bed has started to tick. It's an electronic clock that has *silently* told the time for five years. Now all of the sudden it has decided to tick. So I'm lying here in bed, very awake at 1:30 a.m., listening to the ticking, knowing I have to wake up at 8 a.m.

Babies supposedly love ticking clocks—apparently it reminds them of when they were in the womb. I find it hard to believe that I ever could have been small enough to fit into anything less than the womb of an elephant.

I had a dream last night—a kind of pre-me-historic flashback where I saw myself in the womb, attached to my mother with an umbilical cord. I realize that's as far back in time as I can remember—and it's made me wide awake.

I don't like being reminded I was once inside another person. Yes, I know—it's perfectly natural. Still... This is the kind of thing I think of at 2 a.m., with only six hours until I'm supposed to wake up. It explains a lot, doesn't it?

Of course, it wasn't that long ago (in geological time) that we were all in the womb, and before that, just the cells of our parents. Yet now I'm at an age where my teenage years sometimes feel like ancient history. My father recently told me, "Oh, the next ten years are the best," while last week my 20-year-old nephew complained, "I feel so old," bringing a new meaning to Einstein's theory of relatives.

And the clock is ticking louder. Sometimes I feel like I've lost track of time. Where did this year go? We're all riding on the back of this unruly planet at 67,000 miles per hour and I'm sure I saw that same asteroid a year ago, so we are clearly going around in circles! Where does that get us?

Tick. Tick. It doesn't even "tock" it just Ticks. While I don't pretend to understand Einstein's theory, or how time seems to go slower as you approach the speed of light (and if this is true why don't light bulbs last longer?) we've all experienced how "Time flies when you're having fun," and days we "thought would never end." We're all time travelers, boldly going into the future, our own bodies like clocks that show time not in days, but years.

It hits me that I'm a product of time (so are you). You wouldn't be reading this if, in previous times, people hadn't invented language and alphabets; if there hadn't been time for technology to develop a way to transmit this to you; time for us to be born; time for me to think of this, time to put it in words, time for you to read it.

I'll never fall asleep thinking like this. It's 2:30 now. I am still awake. I sleep better when I don't have to get up at a specific time. I think alarm clocks, taxes and 24-hour news have undermined modern society.

I don't need this alarm. I'll sleep through it anyway. The alarm just becomes part of my dream—as a warning I've entered a restricted zone on a Thermian space ship or something.

I don't want to hear the ticking—it's louder than my own heartbeat. OK, I've just taken the battery out of the clock and now it's silent at last. The hands have stopped moving, but they'll still tell the right time twice a day, right? I will wake up and be glad that the sun rose again and I'm 1,608,000 miles further along my orbit.

FLYING GERMS

Up In The Air, Junior Viruses...

I just flew back from a family reunion in New Mexico, Colorado and Arizona (and boy are my arms tired). The trip was great, but as always seems to happen to me, while I was touring someplace new, the "germs of someplace new" were touring me.

I felt like one of the unfortunate characters at the start of a Dean Koontz novel who contracts a rare and fatal disease by visiting some ancient burial ground (I'd just been to Mesa Verde, the incredible cliff dwellers site in Colorado).

The cliff dwellers all seemed to have mysteriously disappeared at the same time, and I'd just been walking in their old tracks, so who knows what I might have uncovered. While it's all very exciting to think I got this from an ancient race of people, in reality I probably got it from my nephew, Ari, who's a very nice guy, but has a pierced nipple, so who knows where *he's* been.

(My niece, Ocea, would want me to remind you that she's perfect, and that I caught nothing from her except for some new slang. In case you don't know, "Sick" is now mysteriously akin to "Cool." Don't ask me why. My pierced nephew introduced me to "Hard" which is like "Cool" only you have to say "Hard" as if you were a pirate saying "Arrg." And my niece's favorite new phrase is, "That would be at the top of my list if you turned my list upside down.")

So I got on the airplane home—coughing up a storm, wondering if I was going to be the person who starts an epidemic called The Cliff Cough throughout the world.

I hate when *I* sit next to people on a plane who sound like walking germs, and here I was, doing it. So I covered my mouth with a variety of paper goods ranging from the in-flight magazine (which helpfully told me where to buy gold bullion—just what I was wondering about mid-air), to Kleenex and napkins distributed with the peanuts—all in hopes that I wouldn't wind up at the top of a Center for Disease Control chart showing how this new cough began.

To prevent someone from sitting right next to me, I used a trick my flight attendant (and perfect) niece, Ocea, showed me. While the plane was loading, I "Made myself big" and spread out covering 1.5 seats, to discourage anyone from sitting next to me. This worked, so at least there was a small buffer between me, my new-found germs, and the rest of the world.

Luckily it was a short flight, and I wasn't the only one with this cough. This meant at least I didn't start it, I was just carrying it across state lines which, as far as I know, isn't a crime. What was I supposed to do, stay in Arizona until it passed? I know my mother would have liked that, taking care of me like the giant baby she (and my wife) think I am.

And now I'm home, feeling like someone opened spigots in my feet and let all my energy drain out. I've got all the classic achy, feverish, stuffy nose and cough symptoms, as an enduring reminder of my trip (as if I could forget all that family fun).

But don't worry, as far as I know I can't spread germs via e-mail. Yet another reason why the web is a great way to travel.

SIXTH-ISH
SENSE

Sense of Humor

For a while there, I thought I'd lost my sixth sense. No, I don't see dead people. I don't really want to, either, since I hear they have very poor fashion sense. (I don't blame them, it's hard enough to coordinate your accessories in this life so you can go from day to evening—imagine the complexity in the afterlife where you go from dimension to dimension.) No, This is the sixth sense most of us share—a sense of humor. When I lost my glasses I had a hard time seeing—now I had a hard time laughing.

I always used to carry humor with me and it came in awfully handy. I remember laughing all through my wedding—watching our mothers cry. I remember laughing with my sister in my mother's hospital room. Even my mother laughed—it only hurt when she *didn't* laugh.

So after September 11th, I realized my sense of humor had disappeared faster than my hair (and trust me, it's better to be able to laugh about your hair of lack thereof), I started looking for it. My sense of humor, not my hair.

When I lose something I tend to look under the bed first—as if it has some kind of otherworldly gravitational pull. All I could find under the bed was socks. I seem to have some kind of karmic connection with laundry. I can't explain it.

I kept looking. I read a book by a favorite author. I thought I'd found my sense of humor again on page 72, but not quite—it was like when you can almost remember something—you know the letter it starts with, but you can't remember the rest. I tend to think things start with K (supposedly "K" is the funniest letter of the alphabet) then they turn out to have started with an S. It annoys my wife no end.

Maybe I left it in the car. Only a few days ago the glove compartment ate my cell phone. Well, more like swallowed it whole, since no chewing was involved. I knew I'd left it there but now it was gone. Then I heard some rattling in the dash and I could see the phone behind the radio. It was a good trick, but this is a very special phone. Maybe I shouldn't have bought the "stealth" model.

The only way to get it out was to butter it or remove the glove compartment door. I seemed to remember that the phone's warranty was void if it was covered with any kind of dairy product, so I removed the glove box door. It's the kind of thing you look back and laugh at. But I wasn't laughing.

I still hadn't found my sixth sense. After going through the kitchen "junk drawer" and finding only junk, I braced myself to delve into the domain of sofa cushions. This is always a last resort since they have harbored everything from a five-piece place setting to a live lizard. It was a small one (the lizard, not the silverware) and apparently felt very much at home there after sneaking in through the front door. I suspected it was entering a new phase of metamorphosis and was turning into a couch potatophibian.

The lizard was on my wife's side of the sofa (she didn't know about it until now). The lizard, not the side. Yes, we have sides. We got this double-sofa because on a regular sofa, my tiny wife can magically transcend dimensional confines and somehow cover every square inch so I'm left sitting on the arm (the sofa's arm, not hers, she wouldn't sit still for that, but sofas generally do).

My wife's side has had its own metamorphosis—into a new kind of home-office. She works there with her laptop, while watching two VCRs and broadcast TV and talking on the phone at the same time. I am lucky if I can do one thing at a time, and she gets bored unless she's doing about 17.

So I waited until she was temporarily outside, watering plants (something she hasn't figured out how to do yet from Command Central). I picked up the cushion and found no reptiles, no amphibians, not even a mammal. But I did find:

12 pens a drying, 11 pencils dulling, 10 scraps of paper, 9 colored pencils, 8 little tic-tacs, 7 yellow post-its, 6 remote controls and—5 stainless spoons! 4 paperbacks, 3 car keys, 2 TV Guides, and a CD of Ottmar Liebert.

I laughed. And with that, maybe I found what I was looking for, too.

YOUR INNER SANTA

I, Claus

I don't have to tell you it's been a bumpy year. From bizarre elections to a slowing economy to shocking world events. So many things have broken. Lives. Careers. Trust.

I'm lucky because I didn't break this year—I just cracked. At first I thought I'd patch up the crack and go on as I did, using a concrete mix of denial and hope.

Then I noticed I could look through the crack and see something new inside. Something that could emerge, like a chick from an egg. I realized this by accident, the way so many discoveries are made. I did it by looking in the mirror.

Now, I don't look in the mirror often, which, according to my wife, explains why the little hair I have left sometimes looks as it does. It's not because I'm *not* vain—In my early thirties I tried lots of different things to keep from losing my hair and turning gray. Nothing worked—except to stop looking at myself. Then I could imagine I looked the way I felt.

But a few days ago a storm was raging outside, the electricity had gone off and we were plunged back into the 1700s with only candles. And it was in this new light that I saw what I saw in the mirror.

I saw Santa. He looked jolly, and pleasant... and a lot like me. As I stared at his face, I realized it was mine.

It wasn't such a bad face after all. It was like it had finally turned into what I felt. I didn't started out life as a generous person, but I have become one. I'd accepted the Santa inside me and he finally found his way to the surface through that crack.

As a child, I always liked Santa. I mean, what's not to like? He's a snappy dresser. He works great hours and has snazzy rig. Not to mention the fact that he gives good presents. I knew he wasn't "real," but I still wanted to believe in him.

And now I do. Not just in myself, but in everyone who helps other people. We've seen a lot of Santas this year, helping those in need. And while the Scrooges got more press, if you stop and think about it, all over the world we've seen a lot more Santas than Scrooges—a good sign for the future.

So accept the fact you're cracked—let your inner Santa out.

And to all, a good night.

KEEP HOPE
ALIVE

I Hope So...

Little did I know how little I knew. Three years ago I saw a new year coming, and I couldn't envision how it would turn out. I didn't have a dream. I didn't have a plan. I didn't have hope.

That's when I got very sick. I'm not one of those people who think "you make yourself sick," but I do think that I made myself *susceptible* to getting sick. How? I was afraid. No, I was *sore* afraid.

Three years ago, despite my having kept up with the times, having been on the cutting edge and moving my business to the web, the changing economy was putting my long-time clients out of business, things were uncertain, and it took its toll on me.

Looking back on it, my wife says my perception didn't jive with reality, but back then I couldn't see six months ahead, much less 6 years. I couldn't imagine it. I couldn't even day dream it. It was like the world was flat, and I was sailing off the edge. And it was so exhausting that my body couldn't fight what I got. And it just got worse, and worse, and worse.

Instead of having faith that I would get better, I just had fear that I would continue to get worse. I wasn't afraid of dying. I was afraid of not living. I was afraid of letting my family down. I was afraid of not being able to do what I thought I was capable of doing.

I had literally forgotten how to dream. I used to have elaborate, interesting dreams, but during this time I just slept. I used to have entertaining day dreams, but at this point I was *too* realistic. The dreams sank under all the reasons why they were impossible.

As I got sicker, and a dark future looked closer every day, I became angry and envious of other people's enthusiasm and energy. There was one particular commercial where the people were so happy about buying and installing car parts that it made me cry. I wanted to be that excited about a brake shoe—even if it meant wearing one.

Finally I stopped believing I could get well again. My doctors never told me I could. They only said they could cut big parts out of me. Hope didn't seem like an option. Yet every night before bed, my wife would simply say, "Things will be better tomorrow," and that kept a glimmer of hope alive.

That glimmer got me through. Finally a wonderful doctor said "You can be well again." Hope was once again an option, then a direction, then a force, then reality.

I learned that hope is the *only* option. Without hope I have nothing. Hope isn't "wishful thinking" of the "if wishes were horses" variety. Hope is the most powerful force in the universe. Hope is faith—in spirit, nature, science, humanity.

What matters is having hope in the future—hope that we will wake up tomorrow to a better day. Hope *is* the future—the only future worth having.

Around this time of year, when I want to be appreciative that I'm now totally healthy and hopeful about tomorrow, it gets colder, and darker. And despite celebrations, I somehow see more things that seem hopeless. Injustice. Hunger. War. Age-old issues we humans have yet to rise above.

I would have thought that 2000 years AD (or in the year 5761 in the Hebrew calendar) we, as a species, we would have been more together than we are. But that's just an expectation. Expectations usually only lead to disappointment.

At times like this, I know I have a choice now. I can be afraid, or I can be hopeful. I choose hope.

I wish you hope.

TECH- NOLOGY

V-MEN

Vacuuming Doesn't Have To Suck

I like to vacuum. Most men do, if they'll admit to it. There are two reasons why: the first, and most important, is that it involves a machine with an engine. The second is that men are visually motivated animals, as can be readily seen by the magazines we read. Vacuuming is a highly visual pursuit with the kind of instant gratification we men go for.

I mention this because life is really about how you package and sell things and ideas. Men normally don't confess to liking vacuums, but if someone would just package vacuums correctly, they'd be as macho as sports cars and BBQ grills.

If I were the CEO of a vacuum cleaner company I would revolutionize male-pattern-vacuuming by introducing the "riding vacuum." Like the popular "riding lawnmower" this would turn the vacuuming into a vehicle, thereby ensuring its popularity with men.

I'm sure they'd be *so* popular that men wouldn't even allow their female mates to touch the vacuum. "Honey, it's a sophisticated piece of machinery, better leave it to me." Following that success, I'd introduce the riding washer/dryer.

In the mean time, we v-men will have to content ourselves with the biggest, heaviest, loudest silver, red, or black vacuums we can find, with the magic word "turbo" in the name.

I also recommend the bag-less "cyclone" models. First of all, "cyclone" just sounds macho—it makes me imagine those flying cows in the movie Twister. Next, as a man, I can say that while men might change the oil in a vacuum cleaner (if that was possible), we will *never* change a bag because that smacks of housework. Also, these bag-free models have big clear windows that show us how much stuff we've collected and we find this almost embarrassingly exciting. What can I say, it's a primal thing.

Now, I tend to go overboard with these things, but it works for me, and might work for you. My black v-machine (sounds way cooler, doesn't it) has a racing stripe, and a large silver number on it. Mine is #12, for the amps in the motor. "Amps" sounds manly, doesn't it? No? Say it with a sneer and it will.

Next, I recommend getting one of those Tyvek jumpsuits (it's what Fed Ex envelopes are made of). I got mine at the hardware store and it's supposed to be for painting, but if you stick on a few sponsor logos, like Valvoline, Pennzoil, and Rogaine, it becomes a cool (and machine washable) racing suit.

Of course, since you're operating heavy equipment, you should consider protective eye wear to complete the effect. Avoid *tinted* goggles, however, as this can lead to collisions and broken lamps.

Tips for the ladies: First— try to take it for a spin, and if possible, run it into something. This will ensure you are never allowed to use it again. Next—act *fascinated*. If at all possible—look adoringly at him and seriously consider wearing a cheer-leader outfit. The pain of this will be eased considerably if you explain to your man that the outfit *requires* a diamond tennis bracelet.

Finally—whatever you do, never point out something a man missed. You might think you are helping him, but he will inevitably look at it as criticism, get mad, and very well may never use the v-machine again. I'm *not* kidding here.

Guys: Once your V's tricked out, if you start to get bored with flat surfaces, try going off-road—tackle the stairs, that's a real challenge. And get yourself a stop watch so you can have time trials and compete to break your own world's record.

There's a whole untapped market here! I could sell instructions and cones for setting up indoor courses. I could sell small colored pieces of fabric that racers have to suck up to prove they followed the Phase II house-to-house course (complete with a triathalonic outdoor run segment). Then I can charge people for memberships, so they can set up their stats online, and challenge other v-racers to competitions, where the winners get listed as top seeds and losers are known as "suckers."

I can see this going national, then international, with sponsors such as Hoover, Eureka, Dyson, Dirt Devil and

Viagra. Next come the V-Games. Then all remains is turning it into an Olympic eligible sport!

You laugh now—but just wait 'till you are watching the Survivors challenge where they have to vacuum up Roo doo and the winner gets our new V-Pro model with a built in tent!

It's all how you market it. Gentlemen, start your vacuums.

DIGITAL

NERVOUS

BREAKDOWN

Computer Karma

I've always had good computer karma. I don't know if it was because in some previous life I saved a jacquard loom from some Luddite or what, but they've always seemed to like me. Maybe it's because they can't sense any fear or maybe it's because they know I know how to pull their plug. Whatever it is, except for the occasional glitch in the past, I've been very lucky.

But that all changed last week. I ignored a very basic rule my wife had made years ago: "Never install hardware or software after 5 p.m. or on weekends." The reason is because tech support is closed, and many times you can go nuts trying to install something when you could have called tech support and they'd say something like, "Well, of course, you need click your heels together three times and say, "There's no place like Redmond," before that will work."

It was Sunday around 10 p.m. Two strikes against me—except that I'd called and checked and the keyboard maker's tech support line was open, so I felt the rule didn't apply.

Well, if you are a man and have been married more than about six weeks, you should have learned that your wife is always right. I'm not joking, it's not a matter of her thinking she's always right, which of course she does, but of the reality that she is always right, no matter how annoying that may be.

So you can't imagine that I got a whole lot of sympathy, even though if you're a woman who's been married for more than six weeks you should have learned that all men want to hear when they have a problem is, "Poor baby!" Instead, women tend to give advice, which they know is right, but which isn't really appreciated unless its preceded by "poor baby."

As you'll only understand if it's happened to you, when your computer doesn't work, it's like a part of your brain doesn't work. It's as if computers have become our most important tool, and without it, we're like mechanics without a tool chest, painters without brushes, and geniuses with only half a brain.

So, for the moment, I moved my important files to my laptop and I'm back in business again.

Well, kind of. I couldn't move my email, because the new Outlook Express wouldn't import the old Outlook Express' email from a different computer. It was like a new love that didn't want the previous relationship's baggage.

So I go back to work and in all the excitement it was perhaps the first time in ten years I didn't backup the laptop.

So you can guess what happened on Wednesday. I turned on the laptop only to find that the disk seemed to have amnesia. My wife says this was probably caused by the total eclipse of the sun, and who am I to disagree? I have to admit, I took it hard. When things like this happen my first thought is to open a window and hurl the offending item out of it like a very expensive Frisbee. Then I always reconsider when I remember I'll first have to remove the window screen and that involves too much effort.

If you go to Microsoft's website, you'll read "…If you're like thousands of other businesses already using familiar Microsoft tools to help run your company, a digital nervous system is closer than you think." That's what *they* say.

What *I* say is: "…If you're like thousands of other businesses already using familiar Microsoft tools to help run your company, a *digital nervous breakdown* is closer than you think."

So backup. And always listen to your wife.

COMPUTER
HELL

Gateway to Hell

New computers always carry the promise of "faster, faster," and I don't know about you, but I always hope they're going to work *better, better* and I'm usually wrong.

I've been using computers since they cost as much as a house and filled up a whole room. I've owned a computer as soon as they became about the price of a used car. My first "portable" weighed only 35 pounds and I carried it everywhere.

So now it was time to buy yet another new computer (something that seems to happen at least every three years). I decided to go all high-tech and actually buy it online.

I've since bought computers online without any problems, but this first time was traumatic from start to finish.

The company's web site gave me three different prices for the same product and the least expensive quote didn't have an order button—of course! When I called a real live salesperson, they told me the site's low price was wrong, but after 45 minutes of wrangling finally gave it to me for that price.

I was going to be the proud owner of a new computer with more memory and disk space than the space shuttle.

While they charged my credit card within nanoseconds, just as quickly they managed to lose my order. Their site had no record of it. And without a record of it online, I could never follow up with a real person on the phone. So I waited, in limbo, until a very large box arrived at the front door.

The box included a lot of hardware, but absolutely no paperwork, so I still didn't have the magic "customer number" which I needed to talk to anyone in support or even send an e-mail through their site!

I set up the thing and instantly discovered that the CD-ROM drive wasn't working. I'd already had enough—it was time for it to go.

Easier said than done.

Their phone line had the usual forest of phone tree menus. Press 6 to return a laptop. Press 77 to return a mainframe. Press 1955 to return an Edsel. But no where in this huge list where there a mention of returning a desktop computer. Not one—as if it was some kind of alien technology they were unaware of.

I was on the phone for five days. I'm not exaggerating. Unfortunately, they only had 20 minutes of hold music. It sounded like a bad TV commercial for "Classic pop of the 70's." It took a week to start to forget one particular Stevie Nicks song I never wanted to remember in the first place!

It made me think I'd fallen into an nightmare episode of The Twilight Zone where my particular level of hell was to be consigned to listen to hold recordings until the end of time, not realizing that my life is ebbing away while badly recorded voices tell me "your call is important to us," and the "real people" promised to be at the other end never answer, because (as it's revealed in the last 15 seconds of the show) they're all cobweb-covered skeletons wearing operator headsets.

When I did finally reach people they'd say, "I'm sorry, but I can't give you a return number for a desktop." I'd ask, "Do you know who can?" hoping against hope they'd give me a clue, even if it was hidden somewhere in Nostradamus.

But no. Support couldn't help. The laptop people couldn't help (maybe I could have persuaded them if I'd pretended to be the Jolly Green Giant and said "it fits in *my* lap," but I somehow didn't think of it during my endless hours on hold.

After a few days I just started to go nuts. I wondered if this hadn't been their secret plot all along, that it was a conspiracy by the drug companies or the Psychologists Association or *somebody* because they couldn't possibly mean for it to be this bad.

The solution to this was, of course, my wife. After hearing me ranting and realizing there were no sedatives in the house, she got on the phone herself.

She thought it'd be easy. Ha! She was on the phone for two days and got no further than I had. So she called the corporate offices.

I heard her, she was completely calm, just persistent. But apparently she scared the receptionist so much she was connected to a security guard!

In one of those "truth is stranger than fiction" things the security guard was the only person in five days who could help. He said he'd take care of it (which I thought meant he was coming to our house to arrest us) but which really meant that he called somebody and said, "Help these people or they sound like the type that'll come to the home office carrying a cattle prod."

So despite all our technology, the fact is that it still sometimes takes a wife to get something done.

HOW BAD
DESIGN KEPT
ME AWAKE

Vaio Come and Me Wan' Go Home

It's 3 a.m. I'm asleep. And suddenly, I hear something. "Your bah," a broken voice says. I wake up. Why am I hearing voices? Is someone in the room? Am I dreaming?

Instinct takes over. I freeze. Silence. I must have dreamed it. Scenarios bounce around my brain. Burglars. Here to steal this column before it goes out. OK, now I *am* dreaming. I'll go back to sleep.

I'm at that half-asleep point where you sometimes think you're taking a step and losing your balance—and I hear it again, "Your bat e." I'm awake again. What's going on? I'm "bat e"? Maybe I am. I listen again. Nothing. Was my wife talking in her sleep? It sounds like something she might say, but she sleeps as if she's in suspended animation.

I think about getting up, turning on the light. If it's an intruder, maybe I'm better off pretending to be asleep. I can hear my heart beat. I can hear my watch tick. I can hear that high-pitch noise you hear when someone turns on a fluorescent light (but that doesn't count, because I can hear that most of the time even when the lights are out).

I *must* be dreaming. Was it something I ate? Am I just nervous because I haven't written this column yet and don't think readers would appreciate it if I sent them a blank e-mail?

I fall back asleep. I dream I am an e-mail. It's like being "Beamed up" in Star Trek. I hear that familiar sound and I get all sparkly then disappear. For some reason I remember that the beaming up effect was really created by swirling Tang in a water glass.

And then I hear the voice again. "Your batter eis." And I wonder why I'm hearing this. I lay there thinking must have been having that dream about playing baseball in Cuba again.

Now I'm getting annoyed. If there is an intruder in the house why can't they at least be quiet. It's like when I was a kid, at home by myself at night. I'd hear the toilet flush at the other end of the house and wonder if it's a nervous burglar in the house or just our bad plumbing.

I feel around for the flashlight I keep next to the bed in case of emergency. I find a cough drop because it sticks to my hand. I feels something that might be a mouse and decide not to explore any further.

Now I hear a whirring noise. Then the voice again, louder—"Your battery is low," it says. And it all becomes clear. It's my little purple Sony laptop. When its battery gets low (which takes all of about 30 minutes), it doesn't turn itself off to save energy like any smart machine would. Instead, it turns itself *on* just to tell me turn it off. I've heard that technology can keep you up at night, but this is ridiculous.

This is just *one* of the many questionable design decisions made in this little computer. This machine has an anti-ergonomically designed keyboard, and a particularly nasty button right on the side that can both put the machine into a coma from which it rarely awakens and turn it off so you lose everything. When technology goes bad I show it who's boss and unplug it. But in this case, it's not plugged in, so I yank out the battery.

Now I'm awake. I find the pen and paper I keep by the bed and start writing this. Sometimes old technology is a relief.

FEEDBACK

No One's Home

It all started when I e-mailed AOL from the feedback form on their web site. I politely explained my concerns and clicked "send." Their site took me to a page that said, "Although we cannot answer all e-mail personally, be assured that your suggestions and comments are very important to us..." Now—if it was really important, wouldn't they make the time to reply?

Why is it that many sites act as if they don't have to answer e-mail? It would be as if you had a phone number but never had anyone in your company answer the phone. You would never dream of doing that—and yet many sites do just that by not responding to their e-mail.

I figured my e-mail had gone into the great cyber circular filing cabinet in the sky when out of the blue I actually received a reply that read as if it had been written by a computer:

"Dear Daniel,

Hello! :) I am Ste , I would like to thank you for spending the time to write to us. It is my pleasure to assist you regarding any concerns you may have because I highly value your commitment.

I want to thank you personally for writing to us with your thoughts and feelings. I understand you have concerns about the our service. Your opinion makes a difference.

Please accept my apology for any difficulties and frustration you may have experienced with our service. Thanks again for voicing your concerns.   For answers to your questions, please send mail to our corporate offices. The address is: PO Box 10810, Herndon, VA 22070

Thank you very much for your continued support. Have a great day! Your Online Friend, Steve, Customer Care Consultant"

Now that all sounds very personal, which is good. But it didn't answer my concerns at all, and just seemed like a series of almost amusingly generic apologies. And why could I *not* send e-mail to a major web company's corporate office? They *must* be connected to the web.

I wanted to see if this was really a standard reply. So I wrote another note, saying "I am concerned that I cannot e-mail your corporate offices. If they are having difficulty connecting to the internet, I can suggest several good ISPs they could use." The reply began, " Hello! :) I am Mar   , I would like to thank you for spending the time to write to us... The rest of the e-mail was the same as the first one.

Hmmm. I sent two more e-mails, The first said "I am concerned that your company's logo looks like a black hole sucking up the universe. I believe this sends a bad message to the youth of this country."

The second said, "I need your help. My pet chinchilla, Dusty, is having difficulty logging onto your service because the keys on my keyboard are too large for his tiny feet. Is there something you can do about this?"

I received two more identical replies (well, the names changed—though they were always weirdly truncated in the first sentence as if the "mail-merge" somehow cut them off).

I believe that reading and answering your e-mail is part of your *responsibility* as a citizen of the web. It's also good business. And more than that—it can be a useful, interesting, and *valuable* learning experience.

I'm not holding my breath to get a real answer from this company. Besides, my chinchilla really has no problem logging on or answering his email. You'd think AOL could do as well as a small, South American rodent, wouldn't you?

THINK LIKE WATER

Enjoy the Ride

I had the strangest dream last night. I dreamt I was a drop of water. No, not a drip. A drop. I was part of a fast moving river, all movement, excitement, and the occasional fish or rock.

It was winter, and I found myself trying not to get too close to the icy edge lest I become frozen for months while other drops flew by.

I was going faster and faster, and then in an overhead shot (the kind that somehow seems natural in a dream), I could see myself heading towards Niagara Falls.

I loved the fluidity, the speed. I loved being able to find my way into and out of cracks and crevices. All around me billions of droplets were taking a similar trip, but I hardly noticed them. I was too busy enjoying the feel of gravity, pulling me closer and closer to the edge, then finally

   o

     o

       o

         o

           over it.

I felt the weight

        less

           ness

              of the drop,

   momentarily

          becoming   m i s t

                    separate,   flying.

I hit the river with enough force to make a tiny sound that was part of the roar, then I was rushing into a giant concrete pipe. It was dark and it felt faster, harder. It sounded different. Dull but pulsating. I was forced into the giant electric turbine generator. There I was, a drop of water, generating power for the eastern seaboard. It was all pressure and sound and the risk of turning into steam...

————————————I shot out at jet speed—
                       Too hard—Too fast.

Finally, the river I was in slowed. Then stopped. I was now part of a huge, tranquil lake. No movement. No action. No excitement. What I had feared had come true. I thought I would be bored, but it was actually wonderful. I felt like part of the lake instead of just a drop.

I woke up. It was raining. I thought about the raindrops differently.

I had to laugh at how obvious this one was, just in case I might miss the meaning. I was reminded how important it is to remember that we're all part of something bigger. We're not on this planet, we're part of it. We need each other. Alone, we're just a bunch of drops. Together, we're powerful.

The web is the same way. We're not just "on" the web, we're part of it. We all contribute to it, when we create our own sites and just as much when we're the audience for someone else's. Unless we're frozen, we've got to "go with the flow." You can steer, but you can't go upstream.

Since that dream, I try to remember I'm part of something new, fast, and exciting. But rather than feeling like I have to constantly be moving, I try to remember to take some time to sit back and enjoy being a part of something bigger than myself.

Enjoy the ride.

THE ONCE AND
FUTURE WEB

Here's to Your Cardboard Box

This was not my idea of the future. When I grew up, the year 2000 meant colonies on the moon and flying cars and jet packs and four-day work weeks. In my future, there was giant 3-D TV and no one worried about money. The world was all white and silver and everyone had robots that actually did the housework so you could sleep late or eat breakfast while sitting in the pool.

I'm not saying I'm disappointed that things are basically as they were when I was a child 30 years ago, with the addition of more TV channels and the web. I'm just saying it's not what I expected, and maybe that's for the best.

Which is why, when looking forward 30 years, I'm pretty sure it's going to be a whole lot like it is now, except unexpectedly different.

I'm sitting here, outside on a warm sunny day in at the crest of a new millennium at the crack of dawn (OK, 8 a.m., an unnatural time for me to be awake). I'm waiting for a department store's prop department to open it's yearly sale so I can buy decorative yet useless accessories for my house.

I'm typing on a tiny laptop computer, watching two
kids. Inside a large cardboard box. Pretending they're in
a space ship. The little girl, about six, is the captain. Her
little brother, about four, is the stewardess. At least that's
what he said.

So my prediction for the year 2030 is that kids will still
love to play in cardboard boxes, some of the best toys in
the world, because they can be anything.

To me, the web is like a big cardboard box. It can be
anything. It can be your spaceship or your storefront. It
can be where you see the world, or meet friends. It's the
place we can all be six years old and as happy as if we
were in a giant cardboard box.

And that's how I hope we will all view the web. Not
as some giant printing press for money. Not as some
machine for putting people into little demographic boxes
and trying to "upsell" them.

I like money as much as the next guy or gal, but I
don't think the web should *just* be about money. I love
the fact that I get work from around the world through
my web site, but I also love that I can say anything I want
there. I love that it's *my* place in cyberspace.

Maybe it's naïve of me, but I think the web is the
personification of freedom in its truest form.

Well, the two kids have managed to destroy the box.
So are they thinking outside the box? No, they've just
folded themselves up in it. Apparently, a box doesn't

have to be a cube, it can be a triangle, with open ends. Just as much fun.

So here's to your cardboard box, and whatever shape you want to make it. Make the future fit you.

GOOD FROM BAD
Cast Your Net Into the Web

You know how sometimes you just wake up with an idea your head? That just happened to me. I realized that I would not have been writing this today if a lot of things hadn't gone wrong in the past. These were things that seemed bad at the time, but eventually proved to be blessings in disguise.

For example, I wouldn't be writing this now if, eight years ago, someone hadn't stolen a chunk of a book I wrote, and put it in a major magazine. At the time it seemed like a disaster, but it really started a string of good events.

I started to think about all the things that led me to where I am today. Being petrified to go away to the school that accepted me in New York led to meeting my first (and hopefully only) wife. I also wouldn't have met her if her mother hadn't pretended to be sick so she wouldn't leave school and go to Europe as she'd planned (something she wasn't happy about at the time, but if she'd gone, we might never have met).

Living in a bad apartment building and picking up a postcard on the dirty elevator floor led to meeting life long friends. Being too lazy to take a "real" job led to my getting a part in a movie.

Not being able to afford something that cost $100 led to a job where I started writing about computers and I met a fellow writer who's one of my best friends.

Fighting with a PR person who said no one on earth would ever want a laser printer led me to use the seventh LaserJet ever made, and to immediately see the future of desktop publishing. Having a bi-polar boss who liked to scream at his employees and make them take lie detector tests led to my quitting to write my first book.

Having a publisher who "forgot" to pay me my royalties led me to finding a better publisher and publish the first book about desktop publishing with a word processing program which led to my being able to escape from L.A.

More unfortunate incidents with publishers led me to build my own web site, when the web was young. That plagiarism thing led to my meeting an editor, and writing for one of the first big web sites when it started.

Having to endure later editors there who seemed unable to read more than 150 words at a time led me to abandon my biggest source of income, which led to the wonderful chance to do what I'm typing right now.

And If my computer hadn't had a particularly bad crash, which caused me to miss an important deadline I wouldn't have started writing these personal stories. Finally, if I hadn't almost died a few years ago, I might not appreciate everything as much as I do now.

This is how life works—so when we make friends, fall in love or get a great job, it's either an amazing stroke of luck, or part of some plan far too complicated for any of us to understand, much less really control.

And while I sometimes look back and wonder about the road I didn't take, I remember that I my own plans turned out far different (for the better) than I imagined. So my dreams of what might have been might have turned out far different, too, and perhaps for the worse.

Anne Lamott summed it up with a story in her book, "*Crooked Little Heart*,"

"Long ago, there was a farmer who lived in China. One day, several wild horses crashed through the gates of his farm, causing a great deal of damage. "Oh no!" cried the neighbors, "This is terrible news!" The old farmer shrugged, "Bad news, good news—who knows?"

The next day, the horses came back and the farmer's twenty-year-old-son managed to capture one. All the neighbors ran over to admire it, "Oh, how wonderful!" they cried, "What good news!" "Good news, bad news— who knows?" shrugged the farmer.

Several days later, the farmer's son, attempting to break the steed, was thrown and his leg badly broken. The neighbors rushed over, peering at the young man in bed, "Oh, this is awful news!" they cried. The farmer shrugged, "Good news, bad news, who knows?"

A few weeks later, the Chinese army came by, conscripting all the area's young men for war raging in the south. They couldn't take the young man with the broken leg... "

So cast your net out into the web (or your web out into the net) and try to enjoy whatever catch you reel in.

You *never* know where it might lead.

AT THE TONE

Please Leave a Message...

I have five phone lines. I know, it sounds insane at first—especially since up until a few years ago I'd only ever had one. But my wife got tired of the phone being tied up all the time because I was on the web.

I didn't mind it—I liked that the phone wasn't ringing. And I didn't think that she'd mind because she's rarely eager to answer the phone, much less talk into it. But you know how these things go. Within days of her pronouncement, we had another phone line. Now I could be on the web all day, and we could still talk on the phone.

That was all fine and good until *she* got a modem. Now we basically had two modem lines, and no line for talking. You can see what's coming.

My wife always thinks ahead. I think that women are, in general, more forward-thinking than men. If men were smart they'd just get out of their way, stay home and raise the kids, and let the women rule the world.

My wife doesn't disagree with this. In fact, she always tells me if I just go along with whatever she wants, then I'm freed of all responsibility. If something doesn't turn out right, then it was her decision and she can't blame me. (I can't blame her, either, but that's another story.)

To me, giving up most decision-making at home is certainly worth giving up all possible spousal blame.

So she proclaims that we don't just need a third line, we need a third *and* fourth line. I'm wondering if this isn't excessive, and feel a little guilty because now I see why the phone companies keep adding all these new area codes. But I don't want to be responsible if we need a fourth at a later date, so I agree.

Of course, our house wasn't wired for four lines. So the phone installer comes out, crawls around under the house, drills, has to run lines through the garage, where he manages to get them wound into the garage door spring and breaks it so we can't open the garage door for three days and it costs $600 to fix, and then, like magic, we have four lines!

The fifth line *was* my idea. I wanted a cell phone. People think I'm at the leading edge of technology, and in many ways I am, but teenage girls were walking down the street chatting on *HelloKitty* cell phones while I was still searching for pay phones.

Of course, my wife had ideas about this, too—so we had to get one of those Lt. Uhura-like earpiece things so that we didn't hold the cell phone too close to our heads. Still, this made sense to me, since I can imagine that all the radio waves coming out of a cell phone aren't that much different than the radio waves inside a microwave oven and I don't like the idea of a half-baked brain.

I think five phone lines will be enough for the two of us for some time. But I haven't asked my wife, and she very well may have different ideas.

As so often happens, one thing leads to another, and I realized I needed another answering machine. At first I resisted. The last answering machine I bought was expensive and complicated with a big glowing red HAL9000-like button (really). Listening to messages remotely was so complicated I never could remember how. The instruction book said, *"Simply* press *1234 then wait for a beep, then press* 011 then wait for another beep, then press *022 then #." Why, that's simplicity itself!

I looked on the web and found a new all-digital answering machine with more features than I'd ever seen (including a fun talking clock and a stylish semi-transparent blue case) for a big 20 bucks. It's easy to use because it tells me what to do.

OK, so maybe I'm too easily amused. But little things like cheap, smart answering machines give me hope for the future. When computers cost $20 and tell you what to do, we'll be better off—as long as they're not too smart. That, of course, is best left to a spouse.

UNPLUGGED

Turning Off

I have a shocking confession to make: I'm an electricity junky. There, I've admitted it. I need to be somewhere near small holes in the wall where I can plug in something and have it do its thing. When the power goes out I find myself flipping on light switches I know won't work. I can *feel* the lack of energy—I miss the thrill of electrons buzzing around in the walls.

And I'm not alone—even my chinchilla is addicted. I gave him one of those heated rocks that are really meant for reptiles, and it's his best friend. When the power goes out he just seems *sad*.

It's odd to think that in the last 100 years much of the world has become *addicted* to electricity. If you think you aren't, go to the circuit breaker in your house and switch it off. And *no* batteries (they're just canned electricity). Turn off the main water valve if your house has a well. Without power, just try to buy something at any store, including the supermarket. Try to drive without stop lights. Climb six flights or more of stairs in a high rise. Try to send e-mail, surf the web or watch TV. Of course you *can* live without these things, but you'll suffer serious withdrawal pains.

I'll come over and video tape you (since these reality/voyeur shows are so popular, we can call it

"Electric Island") and we'll see how long it takes before you try to knock me out and take possession of the laptop, flashlight, and portable refrigerator I've brought with me. Then you can tape me as I have an *out of battery experience.*

Recently in California, the high-tech capital of the world 33 million Californians were told their power would be shut off for an hour, here or there as if it was a third-world country. California has the 7th largest economy in the world and more computers per capita than anywhere else on the planet.

A year later it turned out that power companies like Enron were secretly and illegally moving electricity out of state to create a crisis that didn't really exist so they could raise prices 700% in a single jump.

But this, along with the fact that the power goes off regularly in parts of Northern California (like on my street!) when it rains shows how tenuous and easily-interrupted our electronic lifeline really is.

I personally have begun to wonder if it isn't just the Universe's way of telling us to slow down.

You see, there could be a good side to being unplugged for a few hours a day. It gives us more time to nap. It's a good excuse to go outside. It's even a good reason for missing deadlines: "I'm sorry, I couldn't do that work, my power was off." It sure beats "my robot dog ate my Zip disk."

More good news—suddenly mundane everyday things, like making toast or washing clothes, turn into naughty luxuries. Yes, I made toast this morning. I'm bad! (Of course, while toasting I also warmed my hands since my thermostat is set to 60.)

And while "turning-off" sounds good, I have to admit I'm grumpy about it. I've been saving energy for years. I don't use air conditioning. I have a low-power LCD computer monitor. This year our power bill shows we're using 25% less power than last year (despite my wife's penchant for heating the bathroom until endangered rainforest creatures could move in and feel right at home.)

Yet I don't get any credit for this. I don't get back any of the power I saved. I know, virtue is its own reward and I'm helping the environment, but even so, once in a while the power company could leave my power on or at least send a fruit basket.

Instead, during our unnecessary "rolling blackouts," I ended up with a $1,500 paperweight on my desk. The "paperweight" is my computer, and it sat there dark and silent while I wrote this with a Fisher Space Pen.

So here are some suggestions to help alleviate this "crisis."

All "stationary" and "spinning" bikes, treadmills and other repetitive equipment in gyms and fitness centers should be attached to generators. The more you use them, the less your membership fee is (since the club makes money selling the power you generate). I mean, otherwise people are just getting all sweaty and creating nothing. This solution also works for kids and rodents (my chinchilla, however, won't run on these little wheels because he's too classy).

Make it a law that all politicians must wear small windmills in front of their mouths. They give off enough hot air to light up the eastern seaboard. In a similar vein, political analysts and stock analysts should also generate power from all their backpedaling.

And for my birthday this year, my friends can all chip in and get me a solar panel. A big one.

NEW MATH

Pop Quiz

Are you keeping up with your e-mail? Here's a test. Don't be afraid, this *won't* go on your permanent record.

This is a story question—I know you didn't like those in school, but you can do it! Plus, the answers are at the end so you can cheat really easily if you want, and no one will be the wiser—including you, because you'll learn nothing if you don't try. One tip, always round up to the quarter hour because in the real world, things are bound to take longer—usually twice as long, but we'll just ignore reality as most tests do.

OK, here goes...

Your site is doing well and people are e-mailing you like crazy. In fact, on average, you receive one e-mail every seven minutes, 24 hours a day (your site's seen all over the world, remember?)

Not all that's useful e-mail, because the mail that arrives every 16 minutes is spam. Unfortunately, your spam filter only catches half of that. It takes 15 seconds to scan an email and delete each one.

You want to answer all your email, but that takes time. At your very fastest, it takes two minutes to answer an e-mail, but to answer it thoroughly and politely (so that people will remember you kindly), it takes at least five minutes. So average that out and figure out how long it takes to answer the e-mail you received today. You also follow $1/10^{th}$ of the links in the e-mails, which takes, on average, five minutes per link (This isn't wasted time, it's educational).

Now, figure out how many new e-mails you've received during this time.

And how long it will take to answer them.

And how many new ones you'll receive while answering those.

Now, calculate what percentage of all the e-mail you've received is spam offering get-rich schemes, home loans, ink jet supplies or x-rated sites? Multiply this by 24 for no particular reason, then enter it on line 19 of form 1041 and ignore this figure.

Finally, if you have an average 8-hour work day, how much time do you have left to do real work? And, how many people got off the train in New Rochelle?

If you figured out that it took between 9 hours and 45 minutes, and 10 hours and 15 minutes to answer all your e-mail, you're close, but you left out the 84 you got while answering the last batch, so basically, trying to answer all your e-mail is kind of like trying to pay off a credit card balance with the minimum payment—it's impossible if you also need to get anything else done— like have a job or a life. It's like one of those time travel conundrums from Star Trek.

If you feel overwhelmed then you need The Happy Valley Virtual Rest Home's program for the "e-mail obsessed and overwhelmed."

STEP 1: Clear out your Inbox. I recommend moving your messages (I had 336 in my inbox) to a new folder, called "old inbox." Easy enough, and it takes just seconds!

STEP 2: Arrange to have all your e-mail sent through the Happy Valley Virtual Rest Home's special "Mailagator" server, which deletes every message immediately. This means your inbox remains pristinely empty, and you are relieved of all that e-mail stress.

Should people call and wonder why you never responded, you can honestly say you never received the message, and there must be something wrong with your e-mail server. You can then give them the HVVRH phone number, which is guaranteed to always be busy.

STEP 3: There is no step three. See how easy it is?

OK, the HVVRH thing is a joke (don't e-mail me for the URL, it doesn't exist!), but the *problem* of answering e-mail is real.

As machines get faster people stay the same speed. As we get more connected more people from around the world can contact us simultaneously yet we can still only have one real conversation at a time,

It doesn't take long before our lives start to seem like the "chocolate factory" episode of "I Love Lucy." Things are coming at us faster than we can handle them. Some chocolate is bound hit the floor (or the fan).

WATCHING A DUTCHMAN TYPE

Static faction

1:30am. I haven't written this column yet. It's Monday morning and it's supposed to go out on in a few hours and I just don't have it. It isn't so much a case of writer's block as it is bad time management and... OK, so it's writer's block.

I'll just write it now... This is it... apparently. It'll be as much a surprise to me as it is to you.

Normally I write about things that have happened in the past two weeks, and things surely must have happened during these past two weeks, but for some reason I can't remember them, which either means my memory is going (if that's the case I won't remember it's going so there's no sense worrying) or it was just so ordinary that looking back all I see is a kind of static.

Or maybe a lot of that static came from webcams. I finally got one and somehow that consumed days, trying to get it to work with other people and looking at myself on my own screen, thinking that the lighting in my office was entirely unsuitable for a web cam and coming to the breakthrough discovery that my head gave off less glare if I wore a hat.

At first the webcam was just a good tool (read: excuse) to try to video conference with friends. My first successful NetMeeting call was with my friend Pete in Australia, halfway across the world. We saw and heard each other from 7,845 miles away (I found that distance by being distracted here: *http://www.indo.com/distance*) and the quality was surprisingly good. His daughter, Holi, told me a joke with the punch line, "Time to get a new pet tiger!" in her charming Australian accent.

I also webcammed with my friend Bruce in New York and my friend Karen in L.A. and just like that old phone company tagline, it was "The next best thing to being there."

I felt like I'd finally stepped into the 21st century. I've been waiting for "PicturePhones" since I first saw one as a child at Disneyland 34 years ago. And here it was at long last—right in my own home office. Amazing.

Then my friend Pete introduced me to webcam software that would enable me to set up a web page and let other people look out my window at the deer who use the yard as a all-you-can-eat salad bar.

The web cam software came with no instructions, and after a few trans-global e-mails I got it working for a few hours, then it stopped working for a few days until I uninstalled and reinstalled everything. No wonder everyone doesn't do it.

In the process I got I sucked into the swirling vortex of other people's web cams. Sites like *www.earthcam.com*, *www.webcam.com*, (not to mention the inevitable expeditions to eBay.com which had nothing to do with web cams and all to do with my inexplicable need to purchase things like a large gold medal in the shape of an Oreo cookie.)

See—just now—right there—that's how it works. I typed the word "eBay," then I had to go there. Forty-five minutes and 90 "wrist watch" items later I'm back.

The thing about all this "research" (read: distraction) is that time just flies by. I had work I should have done this weekend (sorry, Jack, Roger, Ernest, and Consuela) but instead I found myself watching a college student sleep (how very Andy Warhol), then looking for something more interesting than the majority of webcams that seem to show people sitting at their computers looking like zombies.

I mean, how long can you watch a Dutchman type? That's all one guy did. I had a short bout of semi-wonderment at the fact that I could watch a man in Holland sitting at his computer, and after about 10 seconds I thought, "Why am I watching this?"

People are inviting people to watch them but not doing much worth watching. "Mind-numbing" is the phrase that comes to my numb mind.

To be fair (read: I'm not a total slacker), there are many interesting web cams, like the one in Times Square *http://www.earthcam.com/usa/newyork/timessquare* or the one behind the Hollywood Sign *http://www.earthcam.com/usa/california/losangeles/hollywood/cam3.html* or views of the Eiffel Tower *http://www.abcparislive.com* and these of French, Canadian and American animals *http://www-compat.tf1.fr/livecam/animaux_marin.htm*

This weird (and hopefully temporary) addiction reached it's peak today when I realized that five whole hours (or was it days?) had simply vanished and I hadn't written the my column and it was suddenly time for *Alias* on ABC. It's my favorite new show because I love to watch the vivacious yet brooding heroine kick butt, I guess because the butt in question isn't mine—and because she's doing something worth watching!

All this once again proves that technology is only as good as what you do with it. And that despite scientific claims that the universe is expanding, the world is clearly getting smaller.

DAY-

BY-

DAY

IN THE
ALTOGETHER

Au naturalle

I learned a valuable lesson today—never leave your house naked when your doors are locked. It's an obvious lesson, I know, but I guess I'm just one of those people who can only *learn by doing*.

I have a good explanation for how I happened to be on my front deck, au naturalle. I was getting in the shower. Before I could get in, the toilet decided to overflow for no apparent reason. I have a theory about toilets, that they *like* to overflow because normally they don't see your face. When they overflow, they get lots of attention and face time, which explains why they do this on a regular basis. At least that's how it seems to work in my world.

I was in a movie once where I said the line, "I'm good with plumbing, I once stopped up a toilet," and I was very convincing in my reading because the only acting that was required was in the word "once."

Anyway, the toilet was craving attention and overflowed and the only thing I could find to keep the water from running throughout the house was my towel, which I sacrificed for this worthy cause.

Now I had a wet towel to dispose of. I found a bucket (in the bath tub, which sometimes doubles as a storage space) and put the towel in it and carried it out to hang over the railing of the front deck where either it would be carried off by wet raccoons or I'd figure out what to do with it later.

Now, I don't even like to look at my naked body in the mirror—I wouldn't consciously inflict it on others. And since I live in a rural area where no one can see our house from the street I wasn't flashing anyone.

So there I was outside, arranging a very wet towel over the deck railing, when I felt a gust of wind and heard the sickening thud of the front door closing— quiet, but profound. I didn't even try the door—I *knew* I hadn't unlocked it before I went out. I looked around and realized it was just me and the world with nothing in between.

Don't get me wrong, I have no problem with nakedness. If I had a body like Brad Pitt I would be naked as often as possible—even, as Rosie O'Donnell says, "In the frozen food aisle of the supermarket."

But I am more like something *from* the frozen food aisle, with a body not unlike the Pillsbury Dough Boy. It was at that moment I realized that he's appeared naked for over 30 years, wearing nothing more than a hat and a bandana! If his mere nakedness was not enough, every time he appears he's seen with a different women poking him in the abs as he giggles. What kind of message is this sending?

And who else could get away with this? Certainly not me. I'm a chubby white guy but if I appeared wearing only a hat and bandana I'd be arrested faster than you shield your eyes to avoid seeing my crescent rolls.

I snapped out of it when I heard a car coming down the street, and wondered where I could hide if it was the UPS guy, or worse, the Fed Ex gal. I had to get inside. We had a key hidden somewhere—but it was hidden so well I didn't remember where. I recalled something about the back yard and a treasure map with "six paces north, 27 paces east," and something about a "sticky monkey flower bush" (that's its real name). But since I still can't recognize poison oak when I see it, I thought this might be an especially dangerous endeavor.

Just then the wind picked up and the front door opened. All by itself. I guess it had never been locked in the first place! I lunged towards it before the wind could close it again, and kissed the carpet inside. One more important life lesson under my belt (if I had been wearing one).

THESE BOXES HAVE VINTAGE COOKIES

Expiration Dateless

I just ate some antique cookies. I know, true antiques are over 100 years old, so these cookies were just "vintage." They weren't dated (always dangerous), but from the clues I think they were about three years old.

I don't consider three years very old for food—at least packaged food (we had a pumpkin on our fireplace for over a year—but that was decorative as is the Christmas tree we've had up for over four years).

At the British Museum they have some food that was packed with mummies three thousand years ago. I remember reading a card that said the rice and other things could still be eaten—so I was pretty sure someone had tried while everyone else's backs were turned.

While my wife's back was turned I extracted the cookies in question which arrived in a holiday gift basket from a friend. He didn't know they were vintage because the basket was all sealed in plastic. But when I unsealed it and saw that some items had *expired* in three years ago, I figured we were talking vintage food here.

Maybe it was what they call "New Old Stock," which means that it hadn't been used but it was old selling as new. That's a good thing for things like watches. Not a great thing for good gift baskets. Or maybe he got the basket himself some years back and "re-gifted." I don't know the exact provenance of the present and think it would be impolite to ask—or to not at least try the vintage cookies.

I knew the cookies were older than many wines. I knew that some other items in the box were so moldy they looked like something from a horror movie. But I figured that the ones that were sealed would be OK—so I zeroed in on some chocolate covered cookies that looked Belgian but had absolutely no information about where they came from (I thought that was illegal, so maybe the basket was made before these laws).

I opened one box and took a bite of a cookie that looked like it had seen better days. Yes, I know, any sane person would have looked at the cookie, perhaps smelled it and thought, "I don't think so," but not me. I didn't want to be judgmental. I wanted to give the cookie a chance. And besides, we had no other cookies in the house and frankly I was desperate.

I took a bite and it tasted kind of the way tires smell. Since I prefer my cookies to taste like baked goods as opposed to automotive accessories, I threw these away. Normally I put old food outside for the raccoons and skunks, but I'm not one to be cruel to animals.

After this trauma I was able to ignore the other boxes of cookies for weeks. They sat under a chair in the living room. Biding their time. I'm not sure why they stayed there—I can only imagine my wife was afraid to touch them.

But soon I heard them calling my name (though the sound was muffled since it had to come through both a cardboard box and a layer of shiny silver wrapping).

I pulled out one of the plastic-wrapped trays and shook it. I am not sure how I thought I could divine freshness (or lack thereof) from this audible test, but they sounded pretty good.

I tried to unwrap them. The wrapping was of a kind I suspected could be sent on a mission to mars. It was thick silvery plastic, and no matter how hard I tugged I couldn't open it. I learned, years ago that tugging too hard usually leads to cookies all over the room, so I found some scissors and opened them. Half of them were crushed, but they did at least smell like baked goods.

I took a small bite, lest they taste like Michelin Radials, and amazingly, they were good. Very good. *Aged!* There were round chocolate ones, and square chocolate ones, and the best ones were the almond cookies that had long since been reduced to a kind of magic cookie dust.

As I was eating them (a whole half of a box, to be honest), I did think about Peter Pan. Or Captain Hook, actually, and the green birthday cake he had made to poison the Lost Boys. But I hadn't seen any hook marks on the package and I know my friend wouldn't *intentionally* poison me, and besides, they tasted good.

So there, I've admitted it. I'll even admit that I'd consider eating cookies from the Eisenhower administration if they didn't smell like an Edsel. That's just the kind of person I am.

THE OLD FUTURE

A View From Space

Was the future simpler in the past, or was I? When I was a kid everything astronauts did was fascinating. I drank Tang, even though it tasted like slightly tart dishwater because that's what the astronauts drank. I ate the astronaut's "Space Food Sticks," which were kind of like Tootsie Rolls but in different flavors like peanut butter or caramel. I kept waiting for them to come out with "turkey & dressing," or "Salisbury steak" and was surprised when they never did.

It's not like I wanted to go to Mars or even the moon. I've never had any desire to leave this planet before my time. There was just something so "futuristic" about astronauts. So I longed for their special space foam mattress, and at one point, tried to convince my mother to let me sleep inside a huge cardboard tube.

A friend of mine from high school, Ellen, even turned out to be an astronaut on the space shuttle. She was the valedictorian (of course) and brilliant, so no one was really surprised. Afterwards she was casual about it, as if she didn't want to make her friends too jealous that she'd escaped the earth's atmosphere and we hadn't.

So a few years ago, when I saw that space foam again, the future of my past came back to me. The foam's this amazing temperature-sensitive stuff that molds to your own body (which is, of course, better than having it mold to someone else's body).

The foam's also expensive. Now, I try not to let reality stand in my way, especially in the way of a good night's sleep followed by a good afternoon's nap, but my wife didn't like this kind of foam (she doesn't need a reason but she had one—she said it "smelled") so that was pretty much that.

Then I discovered isotonic mattress pads. Just 2" of the magic space foam. Just over $100. It would give me just enough impression of having a space mattress that I was happy and my wife could live with it because, according to her, "it'll air out."

So there I was, sleeping like an astronaut, only with gravity, lying down, wearing far less than a space suit, and without the nausea it turns out astronauts get but never talk about.

Five years pass (imagine the pages flying off a calendar and the screen getting wavy and some moody Moog music). Now my mattress pad has, apparently, conformed to the body of Orson Welles. Not being a genius of Welles' magnitude, it no longer fit me.

So I bought a new one and when I got it home I had the brilliant idea of putting it on top of the old one. I figured this would be even more spacey and it would feel like floating.

I was excited as I lay down and felt myself sinking into it. It was like being on a cloud. For all of about 15 minutes. Then I continued to sink until the foam was up around me as if I'd been steam-rollered into wet cement.

I tried to turn over and couldn't. Then it started getting really hot. I sank deeper. I felt like I was sleeping on a marshmallow being roasted over a campfire.

I tried to roll off the bed, but found myself firmly held in place by four inches of space foam. Maybe this stuff worked better in zero gravity. Or maybe this was the wrong kind of foam. Not NASA at all, but some kind of alien technology designed to trap unsuspecting humans like a Roach Motel—Sleepers go in but they don't come out.

I wouldn't say I started to panic at this point, just that when I finally did claw my way out I kissed the ground—well, the carpet at least.

So here comes another new year where I'm reminded that the future isn't what I expected. After dragging the heavy foam pads around I managed to put my back out. So now I'll be sleeping on the floor.

And I'm still waiting for a Monte Cristo Sandwich-flavored Space Food Stick. Maybe next year.

HOLLYWOOD &
VINES

Wine, Woman and Song

I worked 80 hours in the past four days, while the woman who was telling me what to do went on vacation. I decided I'd earned the afternoon off, and drove to Napa to see a special outdoor dinner and movie.

Napa is nice—but I don't drink wine, so there's not that much to do other than look at grapes, which are lovely for the first few hours, then all mostly look like grapes.

It's considered great fun to drink wine, then drive to another winery where you can drink more wine. I don't understand this form of amusement myself, and think that getting out of Napa alive could, if televised, become a new kind of game show.

Chrysler was sponsoring this film preview, and a tribute to Rita Moreno, an actress who was in the West Side Story and many other movies over the years and is, according to her PR, the only person to have ever won an Oscar, a Tony (for Broadway), a Grammy (for records) and an Emmy (for TV). They sent free tickets to people who'd hounded them for information about the new PT Cruiser car, and since I was one of those people, I got a free invite.

It was all supposed to start at 6:30, and I used mapquest.com to give me directions, and it said it would take two hours to get there. We were there in an hour, arriving unfashionably early, along with the caterers.

It was about 90 degrees Fahrenheit when we got there at 6pm. They gave people as much free wine as they could drink making me realize we'd have to leave before the crowd unless I wanted to test my airbags).

Free wine flowed like water, but I had to pay $1 for apple juice. This makes sense, of course, as apple juice would have to be trucked in, while wine could have been delivered by donkey.

Tables were piled high with copies of Food and Wine magazine, because they were one of the sponsors. Their magazine was filled with useful tidbits of information like how you can make a pizza on a BBQ without creating a fire hazard. Or how the latest trend among the trendiest was a salad made of pigs ears and pigs feet and that people actually ate them because this trendy Australian Chef named Oizzi was so revered. (Really).

The vineyards were beautiful, and the open air theater was located in what used to be the basement of Jack London's stone house, which had burned down before he ever moved in, so now it was just a kind of ruins—big walls with window holes that beautifully framed the views.

They had a Chrysler PT Cruiser there to look at—except that it was locked, because, apparently, even though they invited us they didn't trust us to get in the car. I mean, we might sweat on the leather and suede interior, or spill wine, or who knows—actually decide to buy one, which they didn't really want, since they were already 8 months backordered. And besides, anyone with any sense never buys the first year of any new car model—it's like buying the first version of any software.

I overheard many conversations of people who had bought cars, three months ago, been told they'd get them in six weeks, and now were having to wait eight months. This only made them more excited. So perhaps they'd be eternally excited if the cars simply never arrived.

They'd all bought the car without ever driving it, because it just looked so cute. And there were many near-orgasmic conversations about how you could order a fake "woody" kit, or burl wood dash inserts, and even a tent which attached to the back and then had room for four to sleep in leather-sueded luxury.

Now, it is a cute car, looking kind of a bread delivery truck from the 40's that had been shrunk in the carwash. But buying it without ever driving it would be like buying a house from pictures in real estate magazines. Kind of dicey.

They finally unlocked the car and I sat in it, and it was very nice. Very tall. Very suedey. Clever little picnic table that pops out of the back for those times when you urgently need a picnic table on wheels. The car, which looks big in pictures, is actually quite small—and the whole thing feels like an optical illusion. I wondered, "What next" and imagined 35 clowns and a dog piling out of it.

It was now 7pm. We had been promised a fancy sit down dinner, and now saw some apple baskets filled with bread hard enough to break a Chrysler windshield with. Also some tote bags with green polar fleece blankets with "Chrysler" embroidered on them. I wanted a blanket, even though it was now 85.

Their magazine, being short (and stupid) had lost all interest and I had to use the facilities. I took a little walk through the vineyards and felt it was my personal duty to water the grapes, if you know what I mean. Sometime in the future, a little bit of me will find its way into a fancy wine. And I'm sure I am not the first to think of this.

Then I noticed that they had these extremely modern porta-potties, so I went to take a look. They were on a trailer and were all stainless steel and looked like something aliens might use to store human test subjects. I decided to risk it and go inside, and it was like being transported to the bathroom of a 747. It was all pebble grained beige plastic and a stainless steel sink you could have performed an alien autopsy on.

The toilet was even like the ones on planes, with that weird sucking sound and blue liquid when you flushed. It will tell you just how bored I was that I found this all interesting.

The tiny room had a motion sensor light, so every time you moved it went on, and if you stopped moving you were plunged into darkness, unable to see where the latch was so you couldn't get out without flailing around constantly.

I did manage to escape, and it was still far too light to show a movie outside. By this time people were milling around the baskets of hard bread looking as if they were going to riot. I asked one of the nice young women who wore aprons with "Food and Wine" on them, like some giant, cloned nametag, and they said, yes, we each got a basket, and there was real food in it, and we'd also get blankets.

I went back to find my wife, who's rear had fallen asleep on folding chairs that could have been designed by the Marquis de Sade. I was afraid she'd fallen into some kind of coma from the excitement of it all, and the fact that she'd gotten a tick bite yesterday and now was high on antibiotics. She'd removed the tick by herself, but made it sound as if it was now crawling around inside her and she was soon to be a mutant with extra arms and legs that would make it difficult to shop off the rack.

She wanted to go, and I refused to leave without a blanket. Some of the clone women named "Food and Wine" were now milling about with appetizers. There were roasted figs on foi gras which people were grabbing as if they were the last food on earth. There were tiny daubs of lobster salad that were wonderful, when you could get them, but apparently a blond women named "Food and Wine" didn't like the look of me, and every time I'd look at her she'd look away and walk the other way. I finally followed one of the other "food and wine" women, bribed her with a dollar, and she gave me the whole tray.

The guy who ran the film festival could tell that the invited guests were looking at him as if he was a standing rib roast in a Hawaiian shirt, so he ordered the food baskets be distributed. We'd heard him whispering to his little assistant before the announcement, so we were the first in line, lest they run out of blankets.

The basket of food really was good—a gourmet turkey sandwich on a sour dough roll, a roast beef sandwich on foccacia, two big hard baguettes, a small wheel of goat cheese with a complimentary teak spreader, a half pound of famous local jack cheese, a bunch of tiny champagne grapes (probably containing pee somewhere along the line), a box of orange cookies, and a tin of mints.

Then there was the bag with the blanket which also contained two bottles of wine, a bottle of Evian water large enough to fill the Chrysler PT's radiator, a copy of the stupid Food and Wine magazine we were already bored with, and a stainless steel wine tool that looked like something you could use for one of those porta potty autopsies.

We all ate, which I'm sure saved the life of the film festival organizer. And then we waited. Ms. Moreno was in a group of people who'd paid $90 for dinner that didn't come in a basket, and they were all liquored up in what used to be the barn next door.

It was now 9pm and dark, and the projectionist was making hand shadow animals on the big screen in a desperate attempt to provide some kind of entertainment.

My wife was now sleepy from the tick, the drugs, the heat, the basket dinner, and of course, the excitement. The fog was rolling in, and the temperature dropped to around 50, and the wind was kicking up, so that the movie screen was looking like a sail poised to fall on top of us.

My wife decided we had to go, lest we end up a headline tomorrow, "Rita Moreno, the only women to win an Oscar, Emmy, Tony and Grammy, and 50 frozen onlookers crushed by movie screen at Napa winery"

We did see Ms. Moreno, a very thin woman shivering in the back of the non-Chrysler Town Car that had brought her, apparently waiting for a woman named "Food and Wine" to bring her a blanket.

Meanwhile, we stumbled to the car, which required walking over two hills in total darkness.

I put the top down and we drove the gravel road that ran next to the ruins/theater. I parked where we could see the screen, and we watched like it was a drive-in movie, warm under our new free blanket. The rest of the audience, sitting in those chairs, is going to need thousands of dollars of chiropractic, acupuncture, massage and frost-bite treatment.

But that's a great idea for a film festival—real movies, but at drive-ins. What's better than a fine film, one of those metal speakers that clips on the window, and what passes for Pizza. No champagne grapes, but maybe that would be for the best.

BROILING FOR
DOLLARS

Au Jus!

It all started with fax paper. I needed it for my now antique fax machine which I use in lieu of a copy machine. Yes, I know this is almost absurdly antique of me, but I use my fax machine like a copy machine. So I go to the place I bought the fax machine and they no longer carry fax paper. They laugh at me for still having a fax machine, much less one with the old thermal paper that always rolls itself up like an aromatic hedgehog.

So I go to one of those warehouse-like office supply stores that could double as an aircraft hanger. It's always a mistake for me to go to these places, because inevitably things find their way home that I never intended to buy. Paper in mesmerizing colors. Industrial size packages of pens sporting rubbery grips that will last well into the next millennium.

Being summer, the store is like the inside of the oven. Literally. The ceiling is even covered in some kind of foil, and for a second I have one of those flashes where you temporarily forget where you are and imagine yourself doing the backstroke in au jus, then snuggling up to a potato as if it was a life preserver. I have a sudden craving for a sprig of parsley. Surely that happens to you all the time, too.

I find the fax paper (quite a feat without a Sherpa), then manage to find my way back to civilization—or at least the cash register.

While waiting in a line that appears longer than "Hands Across America," I'm forced to stand irresistibly close to all manner of items I don't need but will inevitably want. I find an item fitting this description—a USB extension cable. This is something I didn't even know existed before entering this oversized easy-bake oven.

Suddenly I cannot live without it. I realize that this piece of plastic and metal will allow me to plug things into my USB port without having to fight my way through a jungle of cables that, in low light, can seem like all those snakes in that Indiana Jones movie. And it's on sale!

By the time I reach the register I feel like I've crossed the Sahara and am so parched I would actually considering drinking a Mountain Dew. The only explanation for this is that I am clearly half-crazed with dehydration.

So when I hand over my credit card and see that $8 fax paper and $15 cable have magically totaled $35, I almost don't notice. And even though my mouth is too dry to speak, I point the cashier to the posted price. Gee,

she's sorry, but she can't give me a refund, I'll have to
trek over to customer service.

By the time the woman behind the counter gets off
the phone I am now at a point where I'd actually pay for
a paper cup filled with tap water. I explain the problem,
walk a half mile under the broiler to where I got the
cable, show her the *two* signs with the sale price, wait
while she tries to explain that the signs are for a different
item, even though the item number is the same and the
only items in sight are the one I was overcharged for.
Then, suddenly she says, "OK, but I don't know how to
fix that."

I start wondering if it's worth $10 to go through this.
The manager arrives, tells her what to do, she takes my
credit card and disappears. I wait, tempted to buy some
more pens, all the while hoping she's not online buying
herself airline tickets.

Then I hear her say, "Oh no!" which is not
encouraging, then "Oh, that's bad," which is even less
encouraging. Finally, she comes back and explains it:
She charged it. Then credited the original charge. Then
credited it a second time, then charged it again. By this
time I don't know if I've gotten my $10 back, or if it's cost
me $10 more.

But since a bottle of fountain pen ink is starting to
look thirst-quenching, and I fear that my wife, sitting in
the car in the sun, will end up unconscious or at the very

least unpleasant from heat frustration I just sign the credit card receipts...

And people wonder why e-commerce keeps growing... e-commerce isn't perfect, but I have to say it's never taken me 30 minutes to check out, all the while being made to feel like a brisket.

AIRPORT
INSECURITY

Close Encounters of the Fourth Kind

They said to be at the airport two hours early—so I was. This was the first time I'd flown since the whole unfortunate incident last year and the first time I felt that security would really be looking for anything in my suitcase other than potentially embarrassing items they could wave in the air for everyone else to see.

Don't get me wrong—I'm thankful they're finally taking this seriously—I just don't understand it when I see reports on the news that someone has gotten a handgun through security when I can't get through wearing a belt.

So I got in a long and winding path to the security check which oddly took just five minutes.

The first thing I noticed was that the security people were tiny. There are plenty of big, tough guys in Oakland, but they had managed to choose people who could have been taken for Keebler elves. Maybe they were chosen so more of them could fit in this small and confined space and the big tough guys were watching from above, ready to throw themselves on you. One could only hope.

There was a big sign with an arrow that simply said, "Here" pointing down at a big hole in a big machine. It had the odd feeling of a Bugs Bunny cartoon, as if this was going to confuse Elmer Fudd into throwing himself into the x-ray machine.

I thought it might not be such a bad idea to lay down on the conveyor belt and get a full-body x-ray. It could save thousands in expensive medical tests and increase the efficiency of the healthcare system. "Take a trip—and a test!" might get more people to the airport.

I resisted getting on the conveyor belt, and put my one piece of carry-on luggage through. The machine promptly spit it out at me as if it tasted bad.

"Ba bop bor bapbop" the woman behind the machine mumbled in a way only a bomb-sniffing dog could hear.

I shrugged my shoulders and raised my hands in the silent international sign of "huh?" and she yelled "Take out your laptop" this time at a volume Jimmy Hoffa could hear.

I thought I'd been so smart when I packed—I'd carry just one bag and it would contain all the clothes and technology I needed. It turned out my laptop, digital camera, chargers, cables and other techno-stuff took up more space than my clothes but I got it to fit.

Now I had to open that bag and take apart the carefully assembled puzzle of clothes and cables it had taken me hours to artfully arrange. I put the laptop in its own little plastic hamper and sent everything through the machine wondering if there'd be any digital information left at the other end.

I walked through the metal detector portal and set off more alarms than you'd hear on P. Diddy's Bentley. Then a tiny man with the metal-detector-wand looked at me as if to say 'is that a rocket launcher in your pocket or...'

He told me to remove my belt, my watch and everything in my 16 cargo pockets as well as my shoes and deposit them all in a tray that was sent speeding down the conveyor belt towards a group of strangers who looked at my tray as if my wallet and shoes would go with their outfits.

Somehow, without anything in my pockets or even a belt to hold up my pants, the metal-detecting wand was still beeping at me as if I'd swallowed a salad fork.

This all culminated with the miniature security man lifting my shirt and waving the wand over my bare stomach while my belt-less pants were inching down and his wand was still beeping. I realized I'd been turned into a floor show for the 120 people now in line and was only embarrassed when there was no applause.

After all this, I got to the gate and realized I had one hour 50 minutes to wait.

After amusing myself by watching what people wore to get on airplanes these days (for a moment I thought I had accidentally stumbled into a sleepover) it was time to board.

Right before walking the plank to the jet, a very large arm pulled me aside and the man attached to the arm informed me that I'd been "selected" for inspection. He made this announcement as if I'd been chosen by Bob Barker on the Price is Right and it was time to "come on down!" What it really meant was I once again had to remove everything from my pockets while they rummaged through my suitcase.

While I knew the small foil-wrapped mint in my pocket couldn't possibly constitute a risk, the security person still eyed me in a way that looked dangerously like he was thinking "cavity search."

Luckily, my iron stomach didn't make his wand beep and I was allowed on the plane, shoes, belt and all. I was relieved to know at least I didn't pose a risk to myself and was fairly secure in the knowledge that no one else had boarded the plane armed with anything more than a mint.

I'M FLYING!

Brave Nut

When's the last time you were weightless? Or head-over-heels? Or flying without an airplane (or chemical substances).

I was upside down 18 times last Tuesday. I went from weightless to experiencing 3G's. I linked arms with a friend and we lived through a 150-foot free-fall without a net.

And you can do it, too.

You don't have to be an astronaut, or sky diver or bungee jumper. You can experience all those things at a place that's probably not too far from you. Since many of us spend a lot of our time sitting at a desk, moving mostly only our hands, sometimes it's good to go out and get all shook up.

And as much as I love the fact that our minds can now go virtually anywhere around the world — it is not the same as strapping yourself down in a roller coaster and doing loop-the-loops and corkscrews.

All of which makes you feel like a cross between a soaring bird and a rat trapped in a washing machine's spin cycle.

At this particular park there was this huge steel arch you could see from all over. Hanging from the arch was one thin metal cable. Occasionally some brave soul would dangle from this thread, be hoisted 153 feet in the air, then dropped, like a stone. They'd swing back and forth in giant arcs like the pendulum of a grandfather clock 15 stories high.

I was there with my niece, Ocea (a very mature 22), and my good friend Pete from Australia. Occasionally we'd stop and look at this thing and wonder who was crazy enough to subject themselves to it. There were no big tracks. No heavy metal supports or braces. Just this thin string, dropping you from the sky. It seemed out of place — too simple.

We watched, up close, while a person turned into a dot. Then we heard a click and they turned into a nut on a string.

Ocea, who wants to be on Survivor (and could be because she's fearless), said, "I'll do it!" Pete and I looked at each other like she was mad. She never looked scared — she just hopped into the harness, walked proudly up to the thing and waved, happily. They hoisted her in the air, dropped her, and she *flew*. When she finally reached earth again she said, "That was awesome!"

I looked at Pete and said "We *need* to do this." Pete looked at me like I was insane and cheerfully said, "OK." We decided to go as a team. We got into the harnesses, walked up to the giant arch (think McDonalds x 100), and kept asking each other, "Why are we doing this?"

Suddenly *we* were the brave-nuts, dangling from the thread, being pulled 17 stories into the air. And it was lovely. It was relaxing. Yes, it was high. Yes we were hanging on by a thread. But the view was beautiful. It was quiet. Peaceful. Not at all scary.

Then we dropped — weightless for a moment — and this, too was beautiful (even though I seem to remember saying "Holy Crap," as we fell).

We were like birds swinging in huge arcs, swooping down just six feet over the grass, then flying up over the trees. It's was wonderful. Back on land, our feet still didn't touch the ground.

It reminded me that things often look a lot scarier than they really are — and sometimes what looks scary is actually bliss. Enjoy the ride.

IT'S
ABOUT
TIME

Time Out

You would never know by looking at me what an exciting life I lead. Last week I had another close call— Yet this dangerous experience seemed oddly normal. At no time was I ever floating above my body, looking down. I saw no white light, well, except maybe for a headlight.

I was driving home and I realized my car wasn't centered on the road. I tried to get back between the lines, but the steering felt loose. Then, in a dream-like way that was all too real, I found that I could turn the steering wheel all I wanted, but it wasn't steering the car. In fact, the wheel spun freely like the red plastic one I had on my crib as a baby.

Luckily I wasn't going too fast. The road sloped to the right towards a ditch, so that's where I went. Better there than if I'd been driving on the freeway, or on a road that tilted into oncoming traffic.

And that was that. Not exciting, just potentially deadly. Maybe I keep having these near-death experiences because I'm a slow learner. My friend Molli suggested that I have them just to prove to myself that someone is watching over me. I like Molli's take better than mine. Either way, I'm once again thankful.

I was fine for two days. Then I got scared. Since then, time has been all out of whack. One example: I realized it was almost the end of the year. I don't know about you, but to me it feels like April.

What I expected to happen overnight has taken a week, and life feels like one of those soap operas where it takes two weeks of shows to get through a single day of story.

When I was a kid, I remember adults saying, "time goes faster as you get older," but I couldn't imagine how that worked. Now here I am, an adult, and I can.

I have a theory about this: When you're young, you haven't lived many days. So each day is a larger percentage of your life. When you get older, you've lived many days, so each day is a smaller percentage of your life.

Do the math: Say you're ten years old. You remember being ten, don't you? If not, stop right now, take a nap or have a peanut butter and jelly sandwich and remember. It wasn't *that* long ago, especially in geologic time.

When you were ten, each day was $1/3,650^{th}$ of your life. At 30 (if you're not 30 yet, just play along, because if you're lucky, you'll be 30, and it will happen before you know it), the days feel only 30% as long as they were at ten. By 40, you've lived 14,600 days, so now each day seems 25% shorter than when you were 30—and it takes about four 40-year-old days to feel like ten-year-old day.

And yet—time is relative. If you've ever been in an accident, then you can remember how time moves in ultra-slow-motion. Maybe if I paid more attention, I could feel time like I did when I was 10.

Before you get depressed, there *is* an up-side to all this. The older you are, the more experiences you have, so the more you can relate to. So at 40, you should be able to understand and appreciate things 400% more than you did when you were ten. At least, that's my theory.

THE YEAR
AHEAD

Seeing Into The Future

I used to want to be able to see into the future. Sometimes I *am* able to see a few hours into the future and know what's going to happen, like when I eat chili, but mostly it's a mystery.

For a while I would read several different horoscopes a day—thinking that if I cross-referenced them and they had something in common then it certainly must be a sign of *some* kind. The kind was, more of than not, a sign written in some language that I couldn't understand, if not a dead language.

So imagine my delight when I received an e-mail from a semi-famous astrologer who offered me "The Year Ahead" as an e-book for only $4.95. It was almost irresistible—almost being the key word here.

I clicked on the link in the e-mail to go to the web site that sold the eBook (and frankly, one of the things wrong with "eBooks" is the name. It doesn't exactly roll off the tongue like "e-mail" or "e-commerce," or "e-tu Brutus." And Book-e has en entirely different meaning—but I digress).

I clicked on my sign (Gemini, the slightly schizo sign) and saw I could save 25 cents by joining a club that cost $25. Wow! Again I resisted.

I read the description, which started, "What surprises does the year have in store for you..." and I thought, "Well, if you tell me it won't be a surprise now, will it?" and that's when it hit me.

I don't *want* to know the year in advance. I want to be blissfully unaware of anything shocking, and pleasantly surprised by anything pleasantly surprising.

I like daily horoscopes that say, "Don't sign any contracts today" on the day they aren't to be signed, because as well as being useful, it makes me feel better that I don't actually *have* any contracts to sign that day.

But do I want to know, six months in advance, that August is going to be a difficult month, full of trials and challenges? Nope. Do I want to know that I can look forward to something November, just so I can get through August? Nope.

My wife tells me that there's a new book out with the premise that worrying is unnatural, that other animals don't worry, and that while fear is a natural and useful feeling, worrying isn't helpful, just draining.

And that's why I'm going to skip the $4.95 year-in-review offer. If the year's bringing good news, then I'll enjoy it as it happens, rather than by so looking forward to it that I miss what's happening now. If it has bad

news—well, I'll get it soon enough and I don't need to
fret about it in advance.

See what a wonderfully healthy attitude I'm
pretending to have?

Of course I'm going to click the link and buy the
eBook and wonder what I was going to do to deserve
what was going to happen in August! Of course I'm
going to worry about what might happen because of
some nebulous warning that could mean anything from
"you're going to back out of your garage and tear the
rear view mirror off your car" (been there, done that,
and I have to say not one single horoscope predicted it),
to "You are going to have a muscle spasm while
trimming your beard and the asymmetrical cut you
make by accident will start a new trend when P.Diddy is
seen wearing it on MTV's new hit show, "Yo Mama."

Or maybe not. Maybe I can wrench control of the
future from astrologers and put it back into my hands. I
can start now, by clicking instead on an electric fondue
pot that can be used for both cheese or chocolate, both
nectars of the gods and my two favorite foods.

That's a much better idea. Unless my horoscope for
today says "don't click on any e-commerce links" or "a
friend will tell you that you smell like cheese—take it as
a compliment or risk losing their friendship."

CRANKY

Abominable

Lately, I've been cranky a lot. "Cranky" is not the word my wife would use, but I prefer it to her word, and besides, her word would have to be bl**ped.

I know I shouldn't feel this way. I'm alive. I'm healthy. I have a place to live, food to eat, and even electricity. A few weeks ago I rode the cable cars in San Francisco at night, and had one of those flashes about how lucky I was to be alive and well and riding an antique transportation device through a scenic city. First I watched the stars. Then I admired the city lights and then immediately felt there were altogether too many city lights, it seemed, during an energy crisis... see, cranky.

And that's how it's been. I'm sure it's some kind of "you've made your bed, now lie in it," except that the problem is I haven't made my bed and I lie in it and then the covers get all bunched up, fall on the floor, and I wake up feeling like the abominable snowman. "Abominable" is the word my wife *should* have used. I'll make a note of it and suggest it to her. I'm sure she'll appreciate it.

It's interesting how I can *know* things, like the fact that I should be writing more in my "appreciation journal" yet find myself complaining about things in my normal journal, then noticing that my hands feel dry and wondering how my keyboard got so dirty (I don't mind that I've typed so much I've worn off the letters "s d e c v n m h l o" and "i" but why does it look like I've been changing the oil on my car, then typing? That can't be good).

Then I read my e-mail and find complaints from three readers who said that what I wrote had nothing to do with anything. Well, it clearly had to do with something, even if it was in a round-about way. How boring to always go from point A to point B without taking a little detour to point Z.

Right now, when the usual "over-reaction-to-everything" we get on the news tells us the web is dead (I like when they tell us that *on* the web itself, with their own animated ads flashing at us), it's easy to think maybe I should quit and move to Montana and raise sheep who get more representation in the US Senate than I do in California (cranky again).

When I start thinking those things, my first piece of advice is to relax and have a cookie. I have had people write and complain that cookies do not solve anything, but those people have clearly lost touch with their inner child (or they don't make very good cookies), while I find it more entertaining to occasionally lose touch with my inner adult.

These people also seem to forget that chocolate is one of the five basic food groups and is very good for you. Don't try to argue with me about it—wouldn't you prefer to believe this, too?

My personal mantra-in-progress is to remember that every day there are more "pundits" in more places claiming to tell me what's happening, and what *will* happen. They do this in a weird corporate crystal-ball way that just sets up self-fulfilling prophecies.

While it's tempting to sit idly by and watch it happen (come to think of it—that's one of the things that has been making me cranky), *I* can decide I'm not going to play that game. I'm going to make up my own game, my own rules, and even design my own game board that works in my favor.

I'm not going to tell anyone else, so they'll think I'm playing their game while they're really playing mine— one in which *they* don't even have a clue as to the rules.

Call this delusional (it's OK—that's what my wife calls it). But it works for me.

INSECTICIDE

Swarming

Last night, a spider the size of an overcoat button was crawling on my wife's leg. At the time it seemed big enough to audition as a Budweiser Clydesdale. I didn't have time to trap it and take it outside as I usually do, so it went to a watery grave, if you know what I mean.

Living in the country, I know there are millions more insects than people. I try not to kill on them, thinking of chaos theory and wondering if stepping on one bug will change history in some small way that becomes huge over time.

I only kill them in self defense and since my wife swells up like a Macy's Thanksgiving day balloon if she gets a spider bite, this was clearly self-defense. Yet it still felt wrong, as if this spider controlled a vast array of insects.

This morning I went outside and saw what looked like a cloud of dust. When I got closer, I could see it was countless flying insects in a primeval holding pattern.

I watched as they landed and shook off their wings, crawling away in pairs stuck together as if they were magnetized. Why would any living thing get rid of its wings? This, too, felt wrong.

The severed wings spiraled into the air, like a tiny
tornado, glistening in the sun, then landing like pine
needles, covering everything, including me. Under my
feet, the blacktop was blacker with ants—no, they were
termites who'd just finished shedding their wings.

I don't think insects have souls. I believe they are
machines that serve the earth. Termites break down
dead wood. What does it say when they crawl on me?

Step by step, I carefully made my way back to the
house without stepping on anything alive. Inside things
seemed normal enough, but then I saw something out of
the corner of my eye. There were a few ants crawling on
the wall, near the ceiling. I ignored them. Then there
was more movement, more ants.

Soon the wall became like a mosaic possessed, with
thousands of tiny spots, forming shapes, moving. They
formed the shape of a bear's head which crawled into
the shape of a 1959 Cadillac Fleetwood before morphing
into a badly rendered Mount Rushmore then melting into
the shape of the state of Florida. It was like watching a
crazed marching band. I was afraid they were going to
start spelling out words. If that happened I planned on
taking a few photos to prove I wasn't insane, then
screaming and running for my life.

I was so fascinated by the shapes I didn't notice that
the white wall had become a dark brown churning
mass. I could think of only one way to control them—I
pulled out the vacuum cleaner and started to suction

them up, watching them whirl around inside the swirling vortex of the vacuum's clear canister.

The ants started to retreat, and soon the wall was white again, no sign they had been there. I couldn't believe I hadn't taken photos. I emptied the vacuum container outside (once again trying not to kill them, just feeling that if they weren't going to pay rent they couldn't live inside).

When I came back inside, there they were again, covering a different wall. I attached the extension hose and tried to vacuum them off the wall again. This time, when they heard the sound of the vacuum, they ran in the other direction as fast as their many little legs would carry them.

I tried to outsmart them by moving the vacuum to the wall where they were headed, but when they'd hear the vacuum, they'd turn back. Waves of insects, outrunning the electricity and technology at my command.

I tried sneaking up on them, having the hose with the crevice attachment near them before turning on the loud machine. This went on for hours, with them regrouping, me sneaking up and suctioning.

Then, as quickly as they arrived, they were gone. The walls were white again, and outside the blacktop was normal black, devoid of wings.

Maybe it was the full moon. Maybe it was Halloween. All I could think of was that just a few hundred feet up in the air, we humans look like termites.

ON FIRE

A True Story

It's midnight. I'm typing an e-mail to a friend when I hear an odd noise; I hear it over and over. At first I think it's the TV downstairs. My wife is watching a tape of "The Amazing Race" and I think she's playing the same bit over and over because I keep hearing the same yelling again and again, and I'm getting annoyed. I go downstairs and watch—no one is yelling.

We live in a rural place where it's usually quiet, so I can't figure out what this noise is. At first I think it's a bird outside. Then maybe kids playing on the street. I hear this voice repeating "Ahhh!" I think it's coming from the hill behind our house.

Finally the voice yells: "Help me!" and I hear what sounds like gunshots. Then they yell "Fire! Fire!" My wife says, "That's what you're supposed to yell if someone is attacking you and you want people to help."

We don't see or smell fire, so I'm wondering what's really going on. I hear more gunshots and wonder if I should hit the floor or begin fashioning a bullet-proof vest out of cookie sheets.

I call 911. They tell me to get more info and call them back! I yell "where are you?" out the window and I hear a woman yell back a street address that's just up the street. I call 911 again.

I yell more questions but the voice outside just keeps yelling "hurry, hurry!" in a way that's loud but not too excited. I hear an explosion and glass breaking so I call 911 yet again. I'm afraid to go out, but I also think I need to do whatever I can. I get out a flashlight and start to run up the street.

I'm running up the street in the dark, feeling like someone in a horror movie who's been told by 911 that the call was coming from upstairs. I'm running towards the disaster like I'm going to be able to do something about it.

I get to the house, and it's glowing—there's a big fire in the kitchen and smoke is billowing out the broken window and all I can think is that it looks like the fake fire in the "Pirates of the Caribbean" ride at Disneyland. I return to reality when the woman inside, a neighbor I know named Melba, is yelling, "I'm trapped!"

And there are more gunshots!

I yell that the fire department is coming, but I can't get in because the fire has reached the front door (and I'm wearing fleece pants that would probably explode in flames if I scratched my leg for too long).

The fire trucks finally come (it was probably only five minutes but it seemed like ages) and I tell them what's going on. By this time the woman has stopped yelling, and I'm afraid she's dead.

Her house is all steel (her husband owned some kind of steel company) and it's basically built on six steel stilts over a creek; none of the house is built on the ground— so of course I'm worried about melting steel and the house crashing into the creek and the fire spreading to the trees and burning down the neighborhood, like the huge fire on the street to the north of us which burned 48 houses in two hours five years ago (that's too many numbers in one sentence, I know).

At first there are two trucks, but only two firemen—as if they weren't quite sure I'd been telling the truth and they didn't want to send out too many firefighters. They also didn't seem too excited about it (of course, it's their job), while I'm feeling like I'm in a movie that's playing in slow motion. They finally break down the door and have to spray the fire with water for a long time before they can even get in. I see lots of smoke and steam coming out.

More neighbors start to appear. The weird part is that we all heard the sound, but all rationalized that it was different things. I thought it was the TV, then a bird, then kids. Melba's next door neighbor thought the sound was coming from the kids on the street below them and went down there to look. The elderly woman a few houses down from us thought it was kids celebrating graduation. No one could tell where the sound was coming from. It didn't seem real.

My neighbor told me she'd known Melba for 20 years and explained that Melba refuses to use the telephone. She won't touch one to receive or make calls. I realize that's why she didn't call 911 herself.

More firemen arrive and the fire's put out and Melba is safe, but is trapped on her back deck and they can't get her out because there's no exit from the deck other than a 42-foot drop to the creek. They set up a big fan to blow smoke out of the house.

I explain this to each new neighbor who appears and wonders what all the trucks are doing there and why the street is blocked and they can't drive to their house.

I meet neighbors I've never met before. I learn one that one of my neighbors is engaged to a woman named Michelle who has a son with a loud motorbike and a ranch north of here. Why am I learning all this now?

I learn from Michelle that Melba has no electricity in her house. I figure if she doesn't like the phone, maybe she doesn't like electricity either. Weird, since I live one house away and practically everything I do requires electricity. I also learn that Melba never throws anything out, so the house is full of newspapers and wood and "lots of steel things" (whatever that means).

Now the firemen are bringing out shotguns, which explains the gun shots I heard—I feel lucky I wasn't accidentally shot by superheated bullets.

I think of our garage, full of stuff, and vow to tell my wife it's a fire hazard. I wonder if there's there some kind of swirling vortex on our street that has attracted people who collect too much stuff.

Now I feel like one of those neighbors you see on the TV news saying, "She was always nice and quiet." She was nice—but actually quite talkative if you got her going.

They bring her out of the house and she's wearing a red plaid Winnie the Pooh nightshirt covered in soot. She's OK. Her dog is missing. She's worried about her guns! I'm grateful I've always been friendly and I didn't even know she had guns.

A fireman tells me that she's alive because of me, and that I may also have saved the neighborhood, but I just feel guilty for not storming into the house in my flammable pants, dodging the bullets and dragging her out.

It's the firemen who really saved the day. Melba's fine, her house hasn't fallen into the creek and her dog was found—so my delay at doing something stupid seems to have been a wise if selfish choice.

And I'm thankful that she finally yelled "help me" and that I heard it because my window was open. It's now 2:30 and the fire trucks are still here.

I'm back at my electric computer, typing this, my sweatshirt smelling a little bit like burnt marshmallows. My window's still open.

MONKEY'S PAW

The Undecided

(I wrote this right before the Gore/Bush "election."
The press kept saying it was going to be practically a tie.
I simply did not and could not believe that. OK, I didn't
want to believe that. I wrote this to subtly scare people
into voting, but in the end, this nightmare came true.)

The moonbeam slashed through the darkness of the
bedroom like a glow-in-the-dark spoon through hot
chocolate. The light seemed unnatural, causing
microscopic specks of dust dancing in mid-air to glow
like the ghosts of atoms gone by.

At first I thought it was a dream—it felt like the inside
a Tim Burton movie. There was no color, just black and
white. I could *feel* the moonlight creep across my face,
as if it was a *thing*. I could look down on myself, and see
my eyes highlighted in a band of clear white light, like a
close-up in an old Joan Crawford movie.

I could hear myself breathing like a stranger. I could
feel the covers pressing me down as if I was a corsage
between the pages of War and Peace. The only things I
could move were my eyes. They moved back and forth,
like a searchlight at a Hollywood premiere—seeing
nothing but night.

And then... I could *feel* a sound. Like Ricky Ricardo
using my ear drums for Babalu. I could feel the tiny

hammers in my head beating out a sound I'd never heard before.

Floup. Ssssp. So loud I wanted to cover my ears, but I couldn't move. Floup. Ssssp. Sharper. Closer. Floup. Ssssp. Time moved glacially. My eyes darted like bats, trying to see where the sound was coming from.

A mouse? No, it sounded more like a miniature kangaroo with a limp. I peered over the edge of the bed. What *was* that thing? My eyes adjusted, nocturnally. It looked like a hand, slapping the ground, then clenching its fingers to move itself. Yeah, right.

It was Halloween eve, so I figured I was dreaming. But if I was dreaming, I'd never think I was dreaming. Would I?

Wait, it wasn't a hand at all... it was a monkey's paw! Then, in a very dream-like way which felt totally real, I was now in a line at the fire station. In line to vote. In my underwear.

I got my ballot and went into the booth. I was ready to mark the ballot when, to my horror, I realized my hand was missing. I couldn't mark my ballot.

It *had* to be a dream, yet it was too real. I could see the linoleum floor, a light gray with black specs. I could hear everyone talking—about the rain, about getting cords of wood for heating. My wet wool sweater smelled slightly sheepish. I could feel myself sweating.

I looked at my ballot, and out of the corner of my right eye, I saw it. The paw was crawling to the ballet, dragging a pencil with it. I was frozen as it climbed onto the ballot. I felt nauseous watching it vote for people I didn't want in office.

Each vote was just one tiny mark, but with each mark I felt my life changing. The world changing. And I was powerless to choose. I realized the paw was brainless. It was just voting for the candidate that the polls had said would win. It didn't care if candidates were qualified, or had a snowball's chance in hell of winning, it just kept ticking them off. Ticking me off, too.

I tried to scream, but no sound came out. I thought about all those people in countries without elections. Those people didn't have a choice—but I did—if only I could do something about this hideous appendage usurping my vote.

I remembered that John F. Kennedy had won over Richard Nixon by *less* than one vote per precinct. What if this paw made that one critical vote? As it crawled out of the booth to place the ballot in the box, I decided I had to do something. I tried to stomp on it, but missed. I tried again, but the paw had dropped a banana peel, and I slipped, hit my head on the linoleum and blacked out.

When I awoke, I had been transmogrified into that most pitiful of all creatures. Yes, I was an "undecided." The future was not mine. I had lost it. Oddly, the election was now a week away, and the TV networks were already predicting the results through their digital crystal balls (after all, why would I want something as mundane as the actual news when I could hear predictions about events that haven't even happened yet from people who had been consistently wrong in the past).

I dreamt I woke in a cold sweat. I couldn't feel my hand. I would have to type this column with my nose and settle for people in office who I couldn't even stand to look at on TV. Luckily, it was only a nightmare. But I had a vague sense of unease that it might come true (except probably for the part about the paw).

Don't let this happen to you. Choose or lose. Make up your mind and vote.

It's not hard. Even a monkey's paw can do it.

IT'S A
LONG
STORY

SUITABLE FOR FRAMING

Where I live

All my life I wanted to live in a magazine page—those perfect pictures of perfect rooms. The sun is always golden, the tables always dusted, fresh flowers always in bloom. Once in a while I'd notice that there was so much furniture in a room there was no place to walk, or that a sofa had been placed right in front of the door, making it impossible to enter or leave the otherwise perfect room. But it didn't matter. It looked like perfection, frozen in time. Always summer. Always the day after the cleaning lady.

My own abodes have tended to look like I lived upstairs from a consignment shop. There was something to look at everywhere, not a flat surface uncovered. From the six-foot-tall purple velvet mannequin with the glass table cantilevered from her midriff to the seven foot round, purely decorative clock face above the fireplace (both formerly window displays from a big department store), to a Christmas tree that was usually up until May . . . my décor was nothing if not eclectic. But it was also nothing like one of those perfect rooms in the magazines.

I always wondered what life would be like in one of those places. No accumulations of magazines and catalogs. No skyscrapers of teetering books. Would you somehow feel more free or be afraid to muss the sofa cushion? Would there be less distractions or would you spend all your time keeping things tidy?

The closest I ever got was having my own picture in a magazine.

It started in our local stationery shop. I'd come into town to get some cough syrup, but the town is so tiny you can walk from one end to the other in less time than it takes to park in most cities. So I parked in the middle, and went in to get one of those roller ball pens with the windows that let you see the ink lolling around, like waves in a bottle.

I was trying to choose between green and purple ink, toying with the wild idea of buying both, when I heard the normally calm proprietress of the store lower the volume on her tiny TV and raise her voice.

"No. I told you before, no taupe."

I'd never heard the proprietress raise her voice before—not even when some kid tried to steal a genuine reproduction of a Babe Ruth baseball card.

"No!" she yelled, her grip on the phone turning her fingers white. "No beige, either. I told you, I have ribbon in white, red, blue and pink. That's all."

I was torn between trying to figure out what her problem was, and adding a red pen to my possible list of choices. I coughed.

"No ecru. No sand. No eggshell. No, no, no. I've told three of you people already, stop calling me!" she spat as she hung up the phone with a force that could have shattered it, had it not been made out of high-impact styrene in the shape of a cable car.

This was the most excitement I'd heard in town since a renegade group of cows got loose from the dairy and ran down the main drag, Highway 1, mooing at the top of their lungs. They might have gotten away without anyone noticing, but all that mooing was hard to ignore, even at noon when the town clock itself mooed.

By this time I'd decided I needed all three pen colors, so I went up to the counter to pay.

"That damned woman," the proprietress sighed.

I coughed.

"She comes into town and suddenly I'm supposed to stock taupe ribbon. First one flunky calls. Then another. At least four have called me now like I could wave a wand and make it appear." (She actually said, "like I could pull it out of my ass," but she probably wouldn't want me quoting her on that.)

"These are $2.99 each, aren't they?" I asked, trying to change the subject.

"I've seen that Martha on TV. 'The perfect potato' or 'the perfect pillow' or 'the perfect piece of toast.' Life's not perfect."

Now I was curious. "Martha Stewart?" I asked, half talking, half coughing.

"That's the one," she answered back, scowling. "People out here only ever need red, white, blue or pink ribbon, so that's what I stock. But no, that's not good enough for *her*."

"Do you know where she is?" I asked, trying to sound casual but coming off as tubercular. The truth was, I was fascinated by Martha Stewart and I had a cough that had my wife calling me "Typhoid Mary," affectionately, of course. I knew a lot of people felt about Martha the same way this woman did, but I personally found her mesmerizing. She presented this dream world where everything could, no, *should* be perfect. And she made it seem as if you could make it yourself, in your spare time, with a pen knife, a hot-glue gun and $200 worth of dried rosebuds.

"Each of them asked if I delivered, like I had wheels for feet."

"Hmm, *where* is she?"

"I don't know, and I don't want to know. I don't have ecru and I don't deliver. That's $9.74."

As I left the building she turned the volume on her TV up again just in time to hear Erica Kane weep, "So what if she wasn't *my* baby!"

My little town, Point Reyes, California, suddenly looked different. It had always projected a sense that time had stopped in the mid-1800's in a small western town. It was charming—not quite Disney-cute, but still rustic like the stage set of a town, just a block long.

I wondered who else Martha's minions had accosted by phone. They should have been calling Toby's Feed Barn, where Chris, Toby's grandson, *surely* would have taupe ribbon. Chris still maintained the feed barn, but had turned the store into an upscale "country" gift shop with items imported from around the world. Chris might even have had ecru ribbon. His dried flower arrangements were, well, Martha-perfect. But I suppose that someone clutching a cell phone, looking desperately in the phone book for ribbon would not think of trying a place called Toby's Feed Barn.

After doing a little more coughing I went over to Toby's and asked Chris if he'd heard anything about Martha. His face flushed. "*She's* in town?" he asked excitedly, his face glowing as if I'd told that the Pope was going to bless his manger.

"So I hear. She was looking for taupe ribbon."

"*I've got taupe.*" He blurted, almost uncontrollably. "I've even got *ecru!*"

"That's what I thought, but her assistants keep calling the card shop." I said, looking at a mug made in Sweden, its matte-glaze feeling like satin under my fingers. "Where do you find this stuff, Chris?"

"All she ever has is red, white, blue and pink. Lord, I knew I should have taken a big display ad in the phone book this year. I could have mentioned ribbons. But everyone here knows I'm here." His eyes were darting back and forth, as if his brain was trying to figure out how to trace a long-over cell phone call so he could personally deliver the ribbon.

"Tell you what," I started, "Give me five yards of both taupe and ecru. If I run into her I can give it to her and then tell you where she is."

He looked at me suspiciously, as if I was just doing this so he might not have enough ribbon left. "Three yards each, that's all. If she wants more, I'll deliver it."

"OK, stay cool," I said, turning away to cough so loud that some of the cow-embroidered flags hanging above our heads started to sway.

I bought the ribbon and personally had a heck of a time telling the taupe from the ecru. I used the red pen to write a little "E" on one and a little "T" on the other, just in case I forgot.

Then I had a quick neck spasm. I knew what that meant. It meant I had to call my wife. We didn't have a cell phone—instead, she just sent out vibes when she

wanted me to call. Either she'd heard about Martha, or
my vibes had sent some sort of message to her vibes,
but one way or another, I would be dead and buried in
the yard if I didn't fill her in.

I walked down to the pharmacy where I needed to
get the prescription filled for my cough syrup and used
the sticky pay phone, the one on the right, the one that
worked. The other had some kind of chewing gum
wrapper in its money slot for the last three years.

"She's in town," I spoke into the phone, first
punctuating my sentence with a cough.

"Martha?" she said.

My wife felt about Martha much as I did—this kind of
dazed awe. The woman certainly was a powerhouse.
We'd been followers since her first book full of pie crusts
too perfect to be real. Pies with faux- grape leaves and
bunches of tiny, perfect doughy grapes. Pies with edges
that looked like they'd had a run-in with pinking shears.
Pies with holes cut in the them in the shape of the fruit
inside. And copper. Lots of copper.

Now, you probably won't believe this, but it's true. My
wife is arguably the world's best (or most annoying)
charades player. You can make one wave with your left
hand and she'll scream, "Gone with the Wind!" No,
that's an easy one, you look to the right and she cries
out, "Look Homeward, Angel!" The best was when I just
had to look the slightest bit constipated for her to yell,

"Titus Andronicus!" So it would have surprised me if she *hadn't* known.

"Yes." Cough. "*The* Martha."

"Where?"

"I don't know—yet." This time I turned away to cough.

"I'd guess the Feed Barn. She'll need ribbon and he's the only place within a 40-mile radius that has taupe," she said, conspiratorially.

"Tried that," I replied, my eyes constantly scanning the road for a blonde in a forest green Range Rover. "Her assistants kept trying to get it from the card shop!"

"Fools!" she hissed. "Call Margaret at Manka's Lodge. That's the only place in the entire county that wraps their bath towels with twine and serves pork chops perfectly roasted in the fireplace."

"I'll do that," I answered, *without* adding, "Like I wouldn't have thought of that."

"No, I call her on the other line, hold on."

She put me on hold while the made-in-Japan combination answering and fax machine insisted on playing hold music that sounded like something you'd hear in a Hello Kitty store in downtown Tokyo.

"I'm back. Margaret hasn't heard anything. Of course she asked me, 'Who's Martha Stewart?' as if she herself wasn't the West Coast version of Martha."

Margaret really was the closest thing to Martha, this side of the San Andreas fault. When she wanted new fencing, she searched for years until she found some freak little forest where all the trees were too close together, so that virtually every trunk was just 4 inches around. She bought the entire little forest, had it all ripped out and turned into what had to be the most beautiful fences—so sweetly rustic, so delicate yet strong, so, well *perfect,* that even the dead trees would have been proud. Her little lodge featured rare $800 Italian brass showerheads, perfect four-poster beds made out of logs and covered in pine boughs, and hand-forged ironwork on the custom-made doors. I'd, watched her look through almost 4,000 typefaces and find none to her liking, so I had to custom design one for her.

There was a pause. I tried not to cough. The only reason I was at the drugstore to pick up the prescription was because my wife told me she would not be responsible for her actions if I continued to cough for one more day. It had been going on for two weeks now and even I was close to putting a plastic bag over my head.

"Johnson's!" I heard buzz in my ear drum, already a little vertiginous from the cough. "The *perfect* oyster! I just *know* it!"

Johnson's Oyster Farm was such an obvious and assured assumption that I was momentarily stunned out of my cough.

"I'm driving out there. You stay in town and keep your eyes and ears open. If you see or hear anything, send me a vibe." She hung up, and I knew she was half way to the car, keys in hand, but purse and license probably still on the kitchen counter.

No matter, my responsibility was basically over. My wife had been notified. She'd figured out the most probable location of the target Martha and she was on her way. Free of obligation, my mind began to wander. I tried to remember just exactly when we had become obsessed with Martha.

When Martha started out, her perfection was a different brand than she sold now. At first she was a type of Hollywood glitz as seen through the lens of a dewy Connecticut morning. It was perfect farm houses and weddings with $500 a head catering which Martha and her magically invisible staff accomplished. Champagne flowed like a waterfall down stacked crystal glasses, gigantic copper trays were filled with hors d'oeuvres that were so small and complex that nuns could have gone blind making them. Her early books were basically big, glossy, full-color, well-typeset ads for Martha's catering business. But they always had a very "don't try this at home, kids," feel to them.

We didn't buy this first book. It was a present. From Spiegel. The catalog company. We'd had some bad encounter with them, I think a box arrived with something living in it, or maybe it was dead, but it wasn't good. They apologized profusely and sent this book, as if the perfection on its pages would rub off on us and better our memories of the folks at 60609 (Chicago's zip code, memorized as a child by watching countless game shows where Spiegel supplied the prizes. They were second only to "Dicker and Dicker of Beverly Hills" in name recognition among the pre-teen set in the Sixties).

We didn't buy her later books, either, we just somehow had them. I think people gave several as gifts, figuring that we were the kind of people who would respond to this. They were right.

Now, our house is far from perfect. Our garage is filled with boxes we haven't unpacked in the nine years since we've moved here. Dust is our friend. Stacks of books and magazines are a prominent decorative motif.

Still, we'd followed Martha's progress, and the real turning point was, for us, her first Thanksgiving special. From that moment forward we were hooked.

She was moving away from the "I'm a genius high-priced caterer" role and into her "I'm your Aunt who knows everything and I'll tell you how to do it, only you'd better do it exactly as I tell you" role. But she still didn't quite understand that not everyone had a refurbished barn/ballroom on their property which was the perfect place to host a thanksgiving for 25 of your nearest friends and their kids and pets.

The Thanksgiving special featured a full tour of her perfect house, called Turkey Hill. It was perfect. Really. It was classic New England white clapboard with green shutters, rolling lawns, stone walls, trellises, even vegetable beds trimmed as if they were high-priced poodles.

We saw her dishes, from the most expensive, to her most charming "tag sale" finds. She had enough dishware to serve the entire population of Bakersfield, with a few bowls left over for the dogs. All of it was fabulous.

But the trick was, Martha wasn't stuffy. She didn't insist on all expensive dishes. She didn't insist that each person's place setting match the next. She had this delightful (to us anyway) eclectic streak, as if everyone could act "old money" and not bother to make things look "model home" perfect, but instead, "rich Aunt" perfect.

This was an intriguing "new" Martha who didn't insist on huge copper trays or imported crystal. This was a Martha who told you that if you could just press a few leaves between two pieces of Belgian linen, sew them up, press them, and paint them around the edges with metallic gold paint you could get at virtually only one craft store in New York City, then place them on the bottom of a stack of books for six weeks until they were perfectly flat, then lay them at a perfect 45 degree angle on each place mat, you would have the perfect napkin. Homemade. At just about $12 each. This was the Martha who brought in a happy man who'd written an entire book just about folding napkins, from those laughable (to him) origami swans and peacocks to minimalist foldings that turned a flat napkin into a burning candle or the dead sea scrolls.

By now my wife and I were staring at the screen, motionless.

Martha went on to show the delicate and rare depression-era glass turkey tureens she was going to use for the pumpkin soup *at the children's table*, ladled out of a real pumpkin with fresh cream from one of the neighbor's cows swirled on top in her initials (you'd use your own initials, of course, she'd grin).

We watched as a set of perfect antique work horses had a pair of perfect antique doors placed on them, and soon this rustic buffet looked like "all you can eat night" at the Vegas Hilton—only tasteful, of course. There was enough food for 25 guests, and a TV crew of two dozen more. At least.

We watched as all the friends and family entered and try to look natural while they knew darn well it was really July and way too hot to wear all that wool and eat a bunch of steaming Thanksgiving fare—all the while being filmed for posterity. Her giant, perfectly groomed Chow dog sat by the door, so motionless you wondered if he'd just come back from a taxidermist. Her giant, perfect coifed Siamese cat walked down the center of the table in a way that would have mortified the health department, though at one point I swear I saw the cat stop at a place setting and straighten the silverware. Unfortunately we weren't taping this, so I couldn't go back to watch an instant replay.

The true piece de resistance was the Turkey. It was the perfect, golden thing, only like the pies in her early books, it was covered with what looked like golden grape leaves and bunches of grapes. Martha smiles as she slices through this pastry crust, a perfectly juicy turkey exposed inside.

Then her mother asks, "What's that, Martha?" as if Martha had taste-tested one too many exotic animals on her poor old mother in the past.

Martha gritted her teeth, smiled and replied, "It's Turkey en Croute, *Mother,*" gently placing some white meat on her mother's plate, then drizzling picture-perfect gravy on it.

The camera cut away before we could see Martha's complete reaction. If it's any indication, we never saw her mother in another shot, though.

From then on, "It's turkey en croute, mother!" became a family joke. We weren't making fun of Martha, really. We knew she was a driven, resourceful, creative, take-no-crap-from-anyone type of woman. We were impressed. Or hypnotized.

Then her magazine, "Martha Stewart Living" started publication. Martha on the cover, tending roses. Martha on the cover wrapping a package. Martha on the cover de-veining shrimp.

We took advantage of the usual "charter subscriber" offer, whereby you get one issue for free, and if you don't absolutely adore it, you write "cancel" on the bill. Then they continue to send you three or four more issues for free, anyway, because their accounting systems are so antiquated.

The magazine was quite breathtaking. Like Martha herself, it wasn't frilly or traditionally feminine. It was as far as you could get from "Victoria" magazine where everything was set in pastels and pages of photographs of lace masqueraded as feature stories.

Martha Stewart Living was slick, elegant, and beautiful, but in a sophisticated, dry, almost cold way. The body typeface was classic, but the headlines were a bold serif that looked almost corporate. The layout was geometric, simple, clean. Lots of pictures anally-arranged like precisely placed packages of potpourri.

It was a look so deceptively simple and powerful that it would come to change the look of many magazines for years to come. It asked readers to come up to its level, at least style-wise. The copy, however, still extolled the virtues of the perfect guest soap. Martha showed you how to make your own candied violets, your own herb forest, your own boxwood centerpiece as if all of us had estates covered with greenery we could just clip and schlep inside.

What Martha never showed you was Rodrigo, or any of her other gardeners or craft designers. Occasionally (more frequently as time passed), she'd introduce you to someone who baked the perfect baguette, someone who decorated the perfect cake, or someone who stuffed the perfect mattress. She was effusive in her praise of these people who had dedicated their lives to perfecting just one thing.

Finally, we broke down and tried to make something she'd made. It was a Grand Marnier orange-flavored brioche oven-baked French toast. We had the Grand Marnier. We even had authentic pure orange extract. We didn't have the brioche, so egg-bread would have to suffice. Of course, you had to start this 18 hours before you intended to eat breakfast. So the day before we assembled all the ingredients, covered and refrigerated. In the morning, we got up early to turn on the oven to bake the thing for an hour at 350 degrees. The resulting concoction was wonderful, and not hard if you just planned your life around it.

Cough—this one so big I thought I was going to lose a lung. It jolted me out of my Martha-induced reverie. I really didn't know how much more of this I could take.

I'd tried all my usual remedies to no avail. I'm sure Martha would have a solution, and if so, my wife would wangle it out of her.

In the mean time, I'd fill this prescription and then stake out the streets of the town (all three of them). The town drugstore has a great sign outside, little colored plastic pieces forming various apothecary things as they might have looked in 1955. How this has remained intact for almost 50 years is a mystery. If only it was back lit and someone could divine a cross in the patterned plastic we could have a holy tourist attraction.

I went inside where they'd recently rearranged all the aisles so that they could see down them to make sure no one was rearranging them behind their backs. Or maybe so they could see the 18 kids who got out of school at 3 o'clock to make sure they weren't trying to hide plastic model kits still unsold from the Seventies under in their way too baggy shorts.

The downside of this new arrangement was that no one knew where anything was, including the two people who worked there. But luckily they hadn't moved the pharmacy area, a raised platform, bathed in greenish-white fluorescent light, in the back. The pharmacist almost glowed in his long doctor-like white polyester jacket. I went back to hand him my prescription, but there was someone else in the way, a *stranger*.

Now, this isn't the kind of town where someone from out-of-town becomes a curiosity. We get enough tourists looking for a rural experience not too far from the city that we're used to it. We even like tourists because they mean our restaurants are actually quite good.

So I didn't look at this guy and think, "tourist," I looked at him, six-foot tall, pressed plaid shirt and pressed khaki shorts *with cuffs*, and pressed socks with perfect caramel-colored suede French hiking boots and I thought, "picture perfect tourist." In our little Old West town if you are wearing two pieces of clothing that are in the same basic color family you are overdressed.

"Stewart," he was saying. I didn't really notice, I was too impressed that anyone could keep a crease on a pair of shorts. I was also trying to keep from coughing, because his cologne, which smelled kind of like an old saddle, an *expensive* old saddle, had irritated my throat.

"Ralph Lauren," I thought, figuring that any cologne that smelled like an old saddle would have to be from Ralph. If it was from Calvin it would smell like the ocean. If it had been cheap it would have had the same "Old Spice," smell that virtually all cheap colognes have, a smell that makes me think of how old men smelled when I was a child.

"Stewart," he repeated, "the doctor at the clinic called it in for an electrical burn."

"Hot glue gun?" I thought. "High-voltage lighting cable?" my brain whirred. Pressed shorts? Had I been temporarily brain-dead?

"Martha Stewart?" I asked, involuntarily.

He nodded, and waved his hand at the pharmacist as if he was the only one on the planet who didn't know who she was because obviously if I, a phlegmatic with wrinkled pants knew her, didn't everyone?

My neck twitched. I didn't dare go to the phone, lest I lose this guy.

"What's (cough) she doing out here?" I asked, causally, as if nonchalance made me seem any less contagious.

"Filming a segment for her series," he replied, turning back to the pharmacist. "I really need this now before we lose the light."

"What's the—cough—topic," I managed to get out, before going into an unseemly coughing fit. I did cover my mouth and look apologetic, but unfortunately I couldn't hear his reply. "I'm sorry," I tried to get him to repeat it, but the pharmacist was handing him the prescription salve.

I wondered if he was going to have to wrap it, or buy a quaint tin to put it in, to make it a bit more elegant and cheerful for her, but he just went to the register to pay.

Now I had to decide between my health, and my life. If I lost this guy my wife would permanently stop making dinner and I might die of starvation after a few months.

I decided I could get the prescription later—right now I had to tail this guy. Unfortunately, even in the best of times I'd make a lousy spy—now my coughing could only have been overlooked by Helen Keller. He looked back at me and I just nodded and tried to appear as if I was going in a different direction.

Martha's preppy-lackey got in his car, a rented minivan with dark tinted windows. I kept a respectable distance. He turned right. I knew it was a bit faster to turn left, go down B street (which is between Main and C, the only other streets in town), then meet up with him as Main turned into Route 1. That way he wouldn't see me following him, and I wouldn't get stuck behind tourists trying to make a left turn to buy bait.

Sure enough, Mr. Pressed Shorts was there, and now I was right behind him. He was driving west, over the San Andreas fault which had moved 20 feet in a single jump during the big San Francisco quake of 1906. He was passing the cow pasture, and the bakery that sold hard, sticky buns baked by a guy everyone called "The Troll." He passed our street, and somehow it seemed unbelievable that Martha had actually driven past our very street. Thoughts like this were making me wonder if I wasn't really an idiot and that ignorance was bliss but I just hadn't figured it out yet.

My wife had to be right—if he kept going in this direction he would end up either driving to the oyster farm, the lighthouse, or into the Pacific Ocean.

Now it occurred to me I hadn't the faintest idea of what I would do if I actually met Martha. I did not have a good record for dealing with celebrities. When I was a teenager I was in a performing group that did shows, often at state fairs in the middle of summer while wearing heavy polyester sweaters, where we were the opening acts for famous people like Milton Berle, Red Skelton, Dinah Shore, and the guy who played Potsie on "Happy Days," and thought he could sing.

I wanted to meet all these people (except the one who played Potsie), so I'd wander the hall right outside their dressing room, just in case they came out—I'd be there, as if I just happened to be there. And I never knew what to say.

So I'd usually end up staring at them for a second (that felt like a minute) and say, "Hi!" That's it. Just "Hi." Like an idiot. Couldn't think of anything else. And they'd usually say, "Hello," or perhaps "Hi," or sometimes they'd turn to their agent or manager or whoever was there with them and say, "What is this kid doing here?"

I remember meeting Dinah Shore. She still had her talk show and I loved her voice. That slow southern drawl made me sleepy. So I waited outside her dressing room, and she came out, and I was there in my heavy polyester sweater. I was basically standing in the middle of a narrow corridor, so she had to either knock me down or say something.

I stood there. Stared at her, and finally said—what else?—"Hi." She looked at me, smiled, and drawled, "Hi," then knocked me over so she could get by. OK, so she didn't knock me over, her manager or agent or flunky did, but I hit the wall with a smack which she probably didn't hear because she was already busy discussing the details of a musical arrangement with her conductor.

So now what was I going to say to Martha? "Hi?" I had to do better than that. "Hello," at the very least. Maybe hand her my business card and tell her I'm available for web site design. Yeah, like that would ever happen. I realized I had nothing to say to her except perhaps, "Turkey, in croute, Mother."

We had entered National Seashore property when suddenly the minivan slowed down, and pulled over. Was he going to confront me for following him? Should I just drive past him? Should I stop and see if he needed help? He stopped. I stopped. He got out and looked at the back tire, now flat.

I figured it was safe to get out of the car, and for a moment, I actually thought I was helping him, until I realized that my ulterior motive was to get him to take me to her.

"Can I help you?" I asked, managing a complete, if short sentence without a cough.

"I hope so, I've got to get this to Martha . . . weren't you at the pharmacy . . ." he said, almost suspiciously, as if I were something out of "Deliverance."

"I live out here, I was just driving home," I lied, effortlessly.

"Oh," I could see he felt guilty about thinking I was stalking him when I was just driving home, or so he thought. "Is the Hog Island Oyster Company out of your way?"

"Just a little," I said honestly, "but that's OK, get in and I'll take you there, it's just about five minutes from here."

"I've just got to get something in the van," he said, running back, grabbing the bag from the pharmacy, then running back to my car. I thought, "Much running. No panting. Must be nice to be 21."

"So you work on the TV show?" I asked casually, feeling the twinge in my neck that told me that my wife was somehow listening to this and I'd better ask the right questions.

"Just starting up, really. We're shooting a bunch of out-of-town segments in advance. Her schedule's so full we have every minute planned, and this is going to make her late." He said, sounding worried.

"I've seen the show." I pretended not to be too interested. "I read she has a temper," I fished. "I also read she backed over a bag of baby chickens, but I didn't believe it."

"I heard that, too. She wouldn't back over chickens. Lighting guys who drop cables and burn her, maybe, but not chickens. She loves chickens." He laughed, then realized what he'd said. "I'm joking, you know."

"Of course." I knew he wasn't, but I wasn't sure if *he* was that lighting guy. "I don't know how she runs a magazine, does a daily TV show, a radio show, writes those books and still manages time to make little flowers out of orange peels." I was sincere.

"I think she's *on* something . . ." he blurted, then covered, "Actually, I've never seen her sleep. Not on planes or driving to or from anyplace. We're all dead-tired and she's still fussing over the placement of a rose petal." He sounded sincere.

"That's amazing, I get tired just taking out the trash," I said, now wondering if we had passed the cut off and if I was destroying this impeccably dressed young man's career in the television industry. I could imagine Martha sputtering into a cell phone, "It's back to selling ties at Nordstrom for you—you'll never work in this business again!"

"Maybe she's superhuman," I said, "you know, like a superhero but instead of a cape, she has a set of draperies made from sheets, edged with silk ribbon from that little place in San Francisco . . . "

"Bellochio. We taped there yesterday," he offered, relaxing. "She had the owner wrap a set of faux $20 pearl earrings in $80 worth of boxes and ribbons. Then she gave it to me for my girlfriend. That was so nice. Now I'm going to get fired."

"Really?"

"No, probably not," he said, sounding a bit disappointed, almost as if it would be a relief if he was. "It's just putting us behind schedule, that's all. I'll probably just have to stay up late braiding seaweed for the photo shoot."

I had no answer for this. I knew *someone* had to do things like braid seaweed for Martha's miraculous magazine, but now I just had the image of this poor preppie, shivering in his neatly pressed khaki shorts, braiding seaweed alone in the dark. Maybe this image of him, alone in the moonlight, might make it into the magazine. Still, I felt sorry for him, even if he did have a full head of hair.

I saw the cutoff to the oyster farm. It's hard to miss, because the entire road is paved in crushed oyster shell, and it gleamed unnaturally white in the sun. As I turned I wondered if perhaps Martha had it steam-cleaned.

Way up ahead I saw a coterie of people in light blues and greens, trucks, lights and a group of overdressed people in tweeds.

As we moved closer, I saw the circle open, and inside, was Martha. It was perfect, as if she were Venus rising from a half-shell of staff—it was so hypnotic I almost forgot to stop the car, until I saw people looking like they'd run away if it didn't mean losing their jobs when Martha got hit by a car instead of them.

As I stopped, my guest jumped out of the car, waved a quick, "Thanks," then ran over to Martha with the salve. She didn't look happy, but she also didn't say anything, she just opened the bag, applied the salve. She clapped her hands and everyone headed towards the beach.

I saw a group of people who were far too well-dressed to be from this area. They were having their picture taken as part of a casual oyster BBQ picnic, but were all dressed as if they're going to a Ralph Lauren's grandson's bris. These people clearly weren't from around here.

I recognized a Latino from town and moved casually towards him. He was wearing long rubber pants, long rubber gloves and a T-shirt that said "Hog Island." He pointed at the people and chuckled, "They're imported from Stinson Beach." I nodded, understandingly.

I noticed a limo and headed toward it. The driver was laying on the hood, his hat on, his shirt off, working on his tan. I knew this guy from somewhere, but I couldn't remember where. Maybe he was a waiter at the Station House Café, or he pumped gas at the Olema Campgrounds. It didn't matter, I'd seen him, he'd seen me, we knew we were locals and they weren't.

"Who are these people?" I asked.

"Heavy drinkers," he said, nodding towards the limo's bar which was littered with empty wine bottles.

"Who?" I said again, hoping this time I'll get a more useful answer.

"Ah, I heard 'em talking—they're friends of some chick named Susie Tompkins…" (The multi-millionaress who started the Esprit clothing line.) "A couple of 'em are people Sammy, the stylist, thought would look good in the picture. She almost used me, but my hair's too long and I wouldn't cut it for some picture in a dumb magazine."

No wonder the pictures of people in the magazine always looked unreal. They are.

In the distance I heard Martha calling for someone named "Thackery." I'd heard this name before—Sean Thackery was some sort of wine expert, creating special blends in his backyard. He led some expensive wine dinners at Margaret's Lodge. The name sounded suspiciously made-up to me. I'd written a cable show years before with a character of the same name which, at the time, everyone told me sounded fake. It felt like the universe was folding around itself and I had somehow become stuck in the middle.

As everyone was being put in their place for the photo I did recognize a few faces, such as the guys who owned the Hog Island Oyster Company. The thin blonde guy was in the front. His hefty, bearded partner and his rotund family were hidden in the back. This really annoyed me. Now I wanted to be in the picture, both to represent the locals and real people everywhere.

The pharmacy preppie was standing far behind Martha, trying desperately to be invisible. But I saw him and approached. I talked fast so I could finish my thought before he could say "no."

"I don't mean to bother you, but do you think you could introduce me to Martha? I'm really impressed by her work and I'd just like to meet her."

He looked at me as if I've asked him to pose naked while braiding seaweed. Then, and I'm not sure if I just imagined this, I saw a little spark in his face, a twinge on his lips, as if this might be just enough to push her over the edge and fire him so he could go back home and join the family business, happy in the knowledge that he didn't really want to be in broadcasting anyway.

"Sure, of course," he said, walking towards Martha. I followed behind him, wondering what on earth I'd say. I heard Martha speak, "Did you forget to turn lights on under the oysters? I want them to *glow.*"

My preppie friend (I started to feel badly that I'd never asked him his name), moved so that Martha could see him, but didn't say a word. He just stood there until she stopped and said "Yes?"

"Martha, this nice gentleman drove me here when the van broke down, and he just wanted to meet you because he admires your work." As he said it I wanted to smack him, because that's just what *I* was going to say. Now what could I say, "Like he said"?

To her credit, Martha snapped into a "public" mode that was instantly warm. She turned, smiled and held out her hand.

Just in time, I remembered to close my mouth which had been gaping open.

Martha said, "Hello and thank you so much for your help."

"Hi," I said.

"I wish I had time to chat," Martha said, "but we're losing the light and need to get this shot in the next few minutes."

"I don't mean to be a bother, but it would be a dream come true if I could be in the picture," I blurted, almost unable to believe I got the words out. I hadn't even thought of it, it just came out of my mouth. I think I was channeling my wife. It was never a dream of *mine* (maybe just a hoot).

The poor preppie looked horror stricken, as if I'd suggested that they put my bald head on the cover of the magazine, thereby frightening small children and household pets.

I studied Martha's face, up close. She was quite a handsome woman, even in person. She was slightly fuzzy, like a peach with professionally applied rouge, and gave off this almost audible buzz of energy. Yet her face gave absolutely no inkling of what she was thinking. It took her a few seconds of looking at me, no, inspecting me, saying nothing. She finally said, "Why of course, stand over there—on the right."

She smiled and now I seemed to detect a combination clock/adding machine ticking in her head, calculating the precise time of sundown and how much this was costing. I didn't mind that—I respected it and went to where she had pointed.

I smiled and was happy to get out of her direct gaze because it was starting to make me feel like an insect under a magnifying glass in the sun.

As I walked towards the group, I realized she'd placed me with the rotund people. No surprise. I got an idea and pulled a pen out of my pocket. Then I saw some young woman wearing a color that can only be described as "pear" pointing me to the right. I went there obediently.

A tree branch snapped in front of my face. I stepped back to hold the branch away, which worked, except that now the tip of the branch was hitting the oyster farmer's wife in the face, something she didn't seem to enjoy.

As I held my arm out to get the branch away from her face, I noticed a few small flashes and heard the

whirring of a motor-driven camera. "Thanks, people."
We were dismissed. The group drifted apart.

I went to look at the table of food, just to admire its
intentionally rustic perfection. The woman in pear
warned me, "They're covered in styling gel and dusting
powder for the picture, you can't eat them," as if just
because of my size I'd automatically planned to eat
everything in sight.

The beautiful people headed towards the limo. I
headed for my car, then turned back to see the crew,
including the pear person, hungrily eating everything on
the table. I looked for Martha, but she had disappeared. I
wondered if I'd just imagined her, but then I
remembered the chilly heat of her gaze.

I was exhausted. All that stalking was tiring. "Crap," I
said out loud—remembering I hadn't given Martha my
business card. "Like it would have mattered," I thought.

It took just a few minutes to drive home, but it was
like leaving one world and entering another. Our home
is wonderful, right on the edge of the woods and the
seashore, but there are bags of mulch in full view, empty
black-plastic planting pots in plain sight, a wood pile
that's falling over and a freshly filled retaining wall that
I'm thinking of nicknaming "Titanic." It doesn't look like
a Martha Stewart photo.

As I drove up the driveway, I saw my wife by the door,
waiting for my report.

"I met her at Hog Island. I shook her hand. I was in a picture for the magazine." I reported, succinctly. "Where were you?"

"I was at *Johnson's* Oyster Farm. I should have known Martha wouldn't take picture of a 96-year-old-man driving his electric scooter around on the beach chasing the illegal aliens!"

"Well, at least you got the oyster part right," I offered, but she was acting like she didn't believe I'd met Martha. "I'll bet you didn't have the camera in the car with you, did you?" she said, accusingly, as if I had claimed to have been abducted by aliens but had no proof.

"I was going to the drugstore when I left, I didn't consider it a photo-op," I said, wearily. Then I remembered my triumph, "But they did take my picture for the magazine!"

"We'll see," was her only response.

So every day when Martha's TV program came on, we both watched, waiting to see what she said about our little town, waiting to see if I'd made it into a picture. Nothing.

Then an episode appeared with Martha in hip waders in our bay, pulling out raw oysters and slurping them down with some kind of chili sauce, the recipe of which was in this month's issue. My honesty was still suspect.

Then the issue arrived. I was not allowed to touch it, of course, because I might smear something. We laid it flat on the table to inspect it without the risk of soiling it and flipped through the pages.

Here was the article. The sunset was much redder than it really was. The oysters were, indeed, glowing. The guests were smiling and laughing, probably because they were happy to be wearing such expensive clothes.

I was starting to get frantic—worried that my picture wouldn't be there and my wife would never believe me again. But there it was—thin people on the left, fat people on the right in the back—not only in the back, but "burned in" so they looked as if they were in the dark, blending in with the trees so that they were almost invisible.

I looked hard, but all I saw was my hand, holding the tree branch. Now my wife really didn't believe me, until she saw, scrawled on my palm, the very light and fuzzy letters "DWH," which I'd written there in a moment inspired by "I Love Lucy" because I had a feeling that, being on the edge, I'd be an easy target for cropping.

I was redeemed. My wife smiled. "Suitable for framing," she said, shaking her head.

It was then I finally realized that Martha lives in a special plane of existence—too *perfect* for reality. One where party guests can be imported for their interesting names or tasteful faces. One where imperfections, such as myself, can easily be removed.

Yet it made me appreciate a whole new world. Not the clinically perfect illusion shown in the flawlessly lit, all-too-carefully-cropped pictures. But in the world *living* right outside the frame—the reality carefully trimmed out of the picture. For better or worse, where I live.

Printed in the United States
17445LVS00001B/90